BIG
SAFE

BIG
SAFE

THE MILWAUKEE CREW
AND THE
RENO REDFIELD HEIST

GAVIN SCHMITT

THE
History
PRESS

Published by The History Press
Charleston, SC
www.historypress.com

First published 2025

Manufactured in the United States

ISBN 9781467156639

Library of Congress Control Number: 2024947394

Notice: The information in this book is true and complete to the best of our knowledge. It is offered without guarantee on the part of the author or The History Press. The author and The History Press disclaim all liability in connection with the use of this book.

CONTENTS

SOURCES AND ACKNOWLEDGEMENTS

Newspaper accounts are the rough draft of history, and that's absolutely true here. Hundreds of articles from dozens of newspapers and countless writers (mostly anonymous) were consulted when putting together the basic framework of this story. Telling an in-depth and coherent tale would have been impossible without these unsung heroes.

The FBI file on the Redfield heist was destroyed decades ago, and whatever threads they pulled on that the police missed cannot be known. I suspect it would have put a spotlight on mystery woman Michaud, but now we'll never know. Luckily, the file on John Triliegi remains largely intact. The Redfield case is not covered in there, but the file provided valuable context for his life.

The Nevada State Library and Archives graciously provided prison records for Triliegi, Gazzigli and Young. Among other things, these files offered the clearest photos of these men from that time. The Wisconsin Historical Society provided the pardon/parole file for Young's time in Waupun State Prison. Thank you to everyone there, especially Deb at the Green Bay ARC.

The University of Nevada provided access to the records of journalist Robert Laxalt, who covered Redfield. A massive, immense thank-you to the Reno Police Department and the City of Reno, particularly Maya Lemus. I made a request for the police file, fully expecting it to have been destroyed decades ago. Instead, I was handed 218 pages of investigative records I'm sure had never seen the light of day before. Seeing the names of informants who were previously unknown was a thrill, and it changed the trajectory of the story—authorities knew some of those involved much sooner than was let on in the newspapers and at trial.

Prison records for Michaud and Giordano were unable to be retrieved. As archivist Stephen Spence explained to me, "The National Archives has inmate files from four federal prisons operating from the early to mid-1900s. Those prisons are Alcatraz, Atlanta, Leavenworth and McNeil Island. The inmate files from every other federal prison have been destroyed. The records from Alderson are gone." An unfortunate situation for anyone researching women in prison, but nothing can be done about that now.

For those looking to read more on Redfield beyond the burglary, Jack Harpster's *The Curious Life of Nevada's LaVere Redfield* is indispensable and available from The History Press. I purposely avoided reading it until late in the process of writing this book to avoid any subconscious plagiarism or even similar outlines. Despite this, I still found gems in there I couldn't find elsewhere. Harpster has written an impressive chronicle of Reno.

Charles Wolf was researched almost entirely through newspapers, though he does come up as a minor figure in the FBI's records on the Bremer kidnapping and the Karpis-Barker gang. I also relied on H. Paul Jeffers's book *Gentleman Gerald*, now out of print. Jeffers plays fast and loose with the facts but left enough crumbs to point me toward where to go. Someone ought to write a new book on Chapman now that finding records and newspaper accounts is easier than ever—some of Jeffers's assumptions can now be corrected. Wolf is also covered in Keith Roysdon and Douglas Walker's *Wicked Muncie* (also from The History Press), which in turn pointed me to Indiana court records available online from the Muncie Public Library.

Emily Schaefer did some excellent background work on LaVere Redfield's family and opened up new research possibilities through newspaper databases previously unknown to me. Her discovery improved not only this book but also all projects I've worked on for the past year or so—and those I'll undertake for many years forward.

Ashley Thiem-Menning, the world's most regal library director, said I could retire after finishing this book. Bram Stoker Award–winning novelist Sarah Read told me I wasn't allowed to retire. They're kind of like the cartoon angel and devil sitting on my shoulders. We'll see what happens.

Bri Lutz and Kait Vondracek kept me caffeinated. In many ways, this is just as important as everything else.

Chelsea Oddwether contributed nothing, but knowing she exists in this world makes it a better place.

INTRODUCTION

Whether or not the Redfield job was the biggest burglary in American history is a matter of debate. In January 1950, the Brinks building in Boston was robbed of an estimated $1.2 million in cash and $1,557,183 in checks, money orders and other securities. That heist was billed as the "crime of the century" and spawned four movies, including *The Brinks Job*, starring Peter Falk and Peter Boyle and directed by William Friedkin, best known for *The Exorcist* and *The French Connection*. Eleven people connected to the caper were arrested, but only $58,000 was ever recovered.

The Reno haul, on the upper estimate, was $2.5 million, a tad shy of Brinks's $2.7. Yet the Redfield heist could be called the biggest burglary on a technicality: the Brinks job was a robbery, not a burglary. Even comparing apples and oranges, though, Redfield is a real contender—putting an exact value on securities provides a great deal of wiggle room. At some point overshadowed by other crimes and largely forgotten, the LaVere Redfield heist in Reno was, in its day, considered the single biggest haul in American history. One officer on the scene remarked, "This makes the Brinks job look like kid stuff." That alone made it significant and newsworthy, but certain aspects of the case that turned up in the investigation made it all the more appealing to inquiring minds.

A key suspect was very much in the mold of the 1940s film noir femme fatale, though a few years too late to star alongside Humphrey Bogart. A little sex mixed in with crime always earns you headlines. There was an interstate and even international component: thousands of miles separated the crooks from their target. If a list of "longest drives to commit a burglary" were ever to be made, this one might top it. In a classic case of no honor among thieves, one crook was soon ripped off by another unrelated person with sticky fingers. And not least of all, the victim was an absolute character. Every step of the way, Redfield spoke and acted contrary to what we expect from those who are suffering a great violation. In fact, he more or less apologized for the crime that was perpetrated on him.

Readers will no doubt be enthralled by the story, as I was when I first heard about it and as many others have been when I've told the tale at speaking engagements. Of all the stories connected to the Milwaukee Mafia (my primary area of research), this one always strikes me as the most cinematic. I can see these characters on the screen of my mind, acting out what seems to me a comedy of errors. Where are the screenwriters and directors lining up to tackle this tale the same way Friedkin did for the Brinks story?

In keeping with that cinematic aspect, the chapters are not strictly chronological. While this story is less complex than a Tarantino plot, each new character will get their own backstory before we catch up with how they fit into the core narrative. The crime itself happened in the blink of an eye, perhaps an hour or less. But those involved are arguably even more interesting than the event they would be forever linked with: a boxer, a dame, two soap salesmen, a handyman, a cocktail waitress and a supporting cast of ne'er-do-wells. As the great comedian Gary Gulman has said, "How often did they do well? Ne'er!"

Chapter 1
THE MARK

Before we introduce our cast of criminals, say hello to our target.
LaVere Redfield was born on October 29, 1897, in Ogden, Utah to William Sheldon Redfield and Sarah Eleanore Browning. He was the baby of the family. William Redfield died at age fifty-two when LaVere was less than two years old, and he likely had no memory of his father. Sarah did not remarry while her children were young, and her occupation on census records is merely "musician," without elaboration. LaVere himself explained that after his father's meager life insurance ran out, Mrs. Redfield supported the family by giving out fifty-cent piano lessons.

LaVere had an interesting bloodline. His paternal lineage traced back numerous generations in the United States but really made its mark when it intersected with Latter-day Saints founder Joseph Smith. The Redfield clan were founding members of the Mormon church and, later, a notable part of the branch group called the Cutlerites in Iowa. LaVere's father was, notably, born in the Mormon city of Nauvoo, Illinois. His other family line was the Brownings, which made the Redfields cousins with the founders of the Browning Arms Company, a gun manufacturer maybe second only to Smith and Wesson. LaVere Redfield himself was not a member of the LDS church, but many in his extended family would maintain their bonds with the influential frontier religion. The Redfield family moved first from Iowa to Nebraska and then to Ogden, around 1891.

As a young man, around 1917, Redfield worked for his brother Fred at the Superior Honey Company in Ogden. At this time, he lived at home with his mother and new stepfather, Thomas Law Whitehill, a salesman in an electric machine concern. LaVere likely could have stayed on in the honey business but soon left to farm potatoes for himself in Idaho Falls. He did not stay at farming long. LaVere would later say simply of his early days, "Life is a gamble." Not every bet pays off, but the only way to win is to not cash in your chips early—try everything.

While LaVere was still a young man, his mother, Sarah, passed in Ogden. This would further crystallize his philosophy of self-reliance, though he certainly had help from his siblings.

By 1919, he had taken up work in Burley, Idaho, as a clerk at the Three Rule Store, and he quickly rose to management by 1920. What brought him there is unknown, as it was a significant distance away from both Ogden (149 miles) and Idaho Falls (125 miles). Court records do show Frederick William Redfield, the same brother mentioned earlier, was an officer of the business, so perhaps this was another instance of LaVere working for Fred. Newspaper accounts show Redfield traveling between Burley and Ogden for business matters connected with the Three Rule Store, which likely kept him in contact with family. While working for Three Rule, he had an assistant named Nell Rae Jones; they soon married in Idaho Falls on September 7, 1922. Nell was a widow, childless and one of Redfield's greatest investments.

Their honeymoon was spent in Los Angeles, and while there, LaVere made a rather large decision on a whim: he invested the few hundred dollars he had in a variety of stocks. The brokerage office he and Nell passed by chance caused a stir in him. "The feverish excitement I saw disturbed me more than I could say," he later told the press. Whether due to luck or business savvy, these choices were the kernel of a savings that ballooned into over $1 million over the next ten years. He later reflected on the moment he realized he was rich.

At first, it frightened me. I had a premonition of things to come, of a change in my way of life, a change made necessary by sudden and tremendous wealth. But then, I realized a strange thing, that I had been foolishly frightened by a common delusion. The fact of money didn't have to change my life. I was in command of the money, and it naturally followed that I was in command of my life. It was so simple that I laughed.

On November 15, 1924, Ogden attorney David Jenson was accused of embezzling $2,000 belonging to several Redfield family members, including LaVere. The act went unpunished for a while because of poor court filings

A rare press photo of LaVere Redfield, captured as he left the courtroom. They hardly, if ever, caught his face on film. *Author collection.*

by the district attorney, with Jenson not appearing in court until September 1926. Jenson was again rebuked in 1928 for mismanaging the estates of Mary Brooks, Otto Johnson and others.

LaVere and Nell moved to Los Angeles suburb Lynwood, California, in 1929. He expanded his investments from stocks to oil wells, including those of dubious entrepreneur Courtney Chauncey "CC" Julian's Julian Petroleum Company. The 1920s were something of a second gold rush for California with the growing oil industry, and Redfield joined at the right time. Furthermore, when Julian's attempts at fraud came to light, Redfield was named a receiver of his holdings. As the Great Depression crippled the nation, Redfield found himself at the peak of his wealth up to that point. (The Julian Petroleum scandal is worth reading more about, if for no other reason than to hear about Charlie Chaplin punching Julian.)

Redfield's motivation to leave Lynwood was simple: he feared that California was on the verge of passing an income tax law. He and Nell moved to Reno around 1935, at which time Redfield was permanently unemployed. The city and state were still in their youth, and a new investment opportunity presented itself: land. His first purchases came from the liquidated assets of eclectic businessman George Wingfield (who we will return to soon), and Redfield now had in his possession at least 25,600 acres in the Tahoe National Forest from the Wingfield acquisition. His land investments also enabled one of his biggest tax schemes: all property was put in the name of "H.B.R. Bushard" (actually his niece Hazel Blanche Warner, Fred Redfield's daughter), with Redfield acting as power of attorney. This shifted the capital gains to Warner, making them taxed at a much lower rate than Redfield would have paid.

At the time Redfield settled there, what made Reno *Reno?*

As the mining boom waned early in the twentieth century, Nevada's centers of political and business activity shifted to the non-mining communities, especially Reno and Las Vegas, which remain the state's two most well-known cities.

The Reno Arch was erected on Virginia Street in 1926 to promote the upcoming Transcontinental Highways Exposition of 1927. The arch included the words "Nevada's Transcontinental Highways Exposition" and the dates of the event. Afterward, the Reno City Council decided to keep the arch as a permanent gateway to downtown, and Mayor Edwin Ewing Roberts asked the citizens of Reno to suggest a slogan for it. No acceptable slogan was received until a one-hundred-dollar prize was offered, and G.A. Burns of Sacramento was declared the winner on March 14, 1929, with "Reno, the Biggest Little City in the World."

Reno took a leap forward when the State of Nevada legalized open gambling on March 19, 1931, along with the passage of even more liberal divorce laws than places such as Hot Springs, Arkansas, offered. The statewide push for legal gaming in Nevada was led by Reno entrepreneur and quasi-gangster William "Bill" Graham, who owned the Bank Club Casino in Reno, on Center Street. No other state offered legalized casino gaming like Nevada's in the 1930s, and casinos such as the Bank Club and the Palace were popular. A few states had legal pari-mutuel horse racing, but no other state had legal casino gambling. In the gaming world, pari-mutuel means a variety of bets and outcomes draw from the same pool—a winner's payoff depends not only on their bet but on how other people placed their wagers on horses, too. Compare this to gambling on the outcome of a football game: once the point spread is determined, there are only two possible outcomes.

The new divorce laws, passed in 1927, allowed people to divorce each other after six weeks of residency instead of six months. People wishing to divorce stayed in hotels, houses or dude ranches. Many local businesses in Reno started catering to these visitors, such as R. Herz & Bro, a jewelry store established in 1885, which now offered ring-resetting services to the recently divorced, and Abe Zetooney's El Cortez Hotel, which was built specifically to cater to the high number of wedded couples seeking divorces in Nevada and was the tallest hotel in Reno at the time of its construction. Most people left Nevada when their divorces were finalized.

Pulitzer Prize–winning journalist Ernie Pyle once wrote in one of his columns, "All the people you saw on the streets in Reno were obviously there to get divorces." In Ayn Rand's 1943 novel *The Fountainhead*, the New York–based protagonist tells a friend, "I am going to Reno," which is taken as a different way of saying, "I am going to divorce my husband" and would have been understood as such by readers of the time.

Within a few years, the Bank Club, owned by George Wingfield (1876–1959), Bill Graham and Jim McKay, was the state's largest employer and the largest casino in the world. Wingfield owned most of the buildings in town that housed gaming and took a percentage of the profits, along with the rent.

He had built an empire in cattle ranching, gold mining and real estate and made more than a few enemies along the way. When he feared miners would strike, he closed the mines, putting eight thousand men out of work in a single day. In addition to the Bank Club, Wingfield also owned the Riverside Hotel, which he financed in 1927 and comes up again in future chapters.

Nevada was able to achieve these laws because it was still very much the "Wild West" and rugged individualism was a strong force. In 1930, the entire state of Nevada had ninety-one thousand people, the lowest population of any state—even lower than Wyoming or Montana, with their vast stretches of undeveloped territory. Convincing millions of people to legalize "vice" was a hard sell, but a few thousand who placed a high value on freedom? Consider it done. (Nevada had actually legalized gambling twice; there was a brief time when Progressive groups managed to make it illegal, but this trend was reversed when other Progressive Era reforms such as Prohibition became unpopular.)

While gaming pioneers such as "Pappy" and Harold Smith of Harold's Club and Bill Harrah of the soon-to-dominate Harrah's Casino set up shop in the 1930s, the war years of the 1940s cemented Reno as the place to play for two decades. Beginning in the 1950s, the need for economic diversification beyond gaming fueled a movement for more lenient business taxation.

Redfield found his "forever home" within a year of settling in Reno: a stone mansion on a hill, overlooking downtown and various pastures, at 370 Mount Rose Street. It was isolated but also within walking distance of anywhere in Reno he would need to go. The house itself was essentially a duplex—two floors of 1,814 square feet each, both with four bedrooms, a kitchen, a living room and two bathrooms. There was also a 1,424-square-foot basement and two garages that were embedded in the hillside. The Redfield couple occupied the entire home, but there are some indications that they largely led separate lives with little in common, and such a house made for an easy division of space. To add to the privacy of the location, LaVere purchased seventeen or eighteen adjoining lots so there was no possibility of new neighbors.

With no full-time job and millions to burn, Redfield took up roulette as a hobby. He knew how contradictory it was to his nature. A man who haggled over nickels simultaneously dropping thousands in one night makes no sense, and yet this was who he was. "Gambling at roulette is pure illogical foolishness," he later said, acknowledging what would appear to most to be a poor investment. "The people who gamble are foolish, and I'm one of them. The only excuse I can give is that I enjoy it as recreation.

And since I have the money, I can afford to indulge in at least one private and expensive habit."

During the first part of the twentieth century, the only casino towns of note were Monte Carlo, which used the traditional single zero French wheel, and Las Vegas, where the slightly modified American double zero wheel was used. The casual player would not recognize the difference, but odds were marginally better for the player on the Monte Carlo wheel. Redfield was keenly aware of this, and as the Monte Carlo variation crept into Reno, he gravitated in that direction and adjusted his system accordingly.

According to author Jack Harpster, the defining day in Redfield's life may have been January 15, 1948. That afternoon, walking home from Harolds Club with $2,300 in a paper bag, he was assaulted by a mugger. The man demanded the money, knowing exactly what Redfield had, but Redfield refused. Most people would probably turn over the cash, and in this case, it was a fraction of 1 percent of what Redfield was worth—equivalent to pennies for the rest of us. Yet he refused and held on even after repeated blows to the head. Redfield, skull fractured, spent the next few weeks in hospital, but he never let go of the money. Nell Redfield would point to this beating as the moment Redfield went from being an investor and collector to a hoarder, collecting without any real aim or purpose.

When the census taker came around in 1950, LaVere said he was retired. Pressed for his former line of work, he told the taker he had been the owner/manager of a dry goods store. Though he was "retired" from any sort of regular employment, Redfield was active in overseeing his investments in Nevada and California. One could also say he was employed as a gambler, though it is hard to call something a career if you often lose more than you earn.

And his watering hole of choice was the Riverside, operated by the questionable Mert Wertheimer, who had made a name for himself as a gambling boss in Detroit alongside the notorious Purple Gang. Learning a bit more about Wertheimer and his friends will help us better understand the gaming atmosphere around Reno, which had a surprisingly high percentage of Detroit men in charge.

Chapter 2
THE VENUE

A s gamblers, Al, Mert and Lou became almost as well-known Detroiters as the automobile pioneers. However, the only thing the Wertheimers built was their reputation as being fabulous spenders and operators of plush gambling establishments here and in other cities," wrote Ken McCormick in the *Detroit Free Press* (June 9, 1953).

To understand the casino scene in Reno, we have to go back in time and hundreds of miles east to Detroit. This was the place where Reno's greatest casino owners cut their teeth.

Mert Wertheimer came up in the casino business in the usual way for men of his generation: starting out in illegal gambling elsewhere in the country and then migrating to Nevada later in life. One should not be surprised Las Vegas and the Mafia were synonymous for so long. Who else had the skill set to take bets, set the odds and so forth? Organized crime had been doing these very things and training others to do it for them for decades. Reno never had the full-blown Mafia culture that Vegas did, but it was there just below the surface.

Born Myrton Wertheimer on June 12, 1884, he was universally known as Mert, and even the newspapers preferred this four-letter word to his full name. Mert ran a clothing store in Cheboygan, Michigan, along with his family and was a high-ranking member of the local Elks Club. He took over management of the store from his father, John, who in turn had taken over from his father, Isaac. After 1917, Mert moved to Detroit and fell in with the gambling element there. What precipitated this change in careers is not known.

The Detroit gambling syndicate really took off in 1915, not long before Wertheimer arrived. Frank Hibbler had a booming gambling resort thanks to the explosive growth in the city's automotive industry. Assembly line workers were ready to spend their earnings at Hibbler's place. Needing more men to run his games, he brought in George Pembroke Weinbrenner (known as St. Louis Dutch) and Daniel W. "Danny" Sullivan from St. Louis. They, in turn, brought in Lincoln Fitzgerald, described by those who knew him as a quiet, "short, pudgy little man." Weinbrenner further aligned himself with the local gambling element by marrying the daughter of local legend John "Bald Jack" Ryan. Again, what linked Wertheimer to these men is unclear, but before long, his name was always mentioned alongside Sullivan's and Fitzgerald's, as it would be for decades.

Wertheimer and his friend Raymond Reuben "Ruby" Mathis opened the Colonial Billiard Parlor in 1923: a pool room with twenty tables on the fourth floor of the Colonial Building at 113 State Street that included a restaurant for refreshment, where gentlemen could hang out for hours on end. The establishment also catered to the gambling community, and by September that first year, Wertheimer had been picked up for keeping a gambling house.

Wertheimer's attorney, Percy Wylie Grose, managed to delay the trial nearly a year, securing no fewer than twenty adjournments by June 1924. He tried every tactic to get the case tossed out. Grose said Wertheimer's arrest was illegal and the seizure of gambling paraphernalia improper because the police had no search warrant. Grose argued on

LINCOLN FITZGERALD

DANNY SULLIVAN

Top: "Bulletproof" Lincoln Fitzgerald, arguably the most successful gambler to come out of Detroit. *From the* Detroit Free Press.

Bottom: Danny Sullivan, a Wertheimer associate who found himself a constant target of the IRS. *From the* Detroit Free Press.

The Colonial Billiard Parlor was Mert Wertheimer's first big outing in the gambling world. *From the* Miami Herald.

September 8, 1923, that the current anti-gambling law was unconstitutional. Judge Frank Murphy rejected all motions, determined to bring the defendant before him in court. A police "raid" required no warrant if the establishment was open to the public and illegal materials were in plain sight. He further cited Michigan's Justice Thomas McIntyre Cooley (1824–1898) to support the legality of the law, noting, "Gambling is not only harmful in itself, but makes for the loss of thrift and absence from one's business, social and domestic duties."

Mert's brother Lionel Abraham Wertheimer moved to Muncie, eastern Indiana, and continued in the retail clothing business. He was assistant manager of the Hub department store under Irvin Goldberg at 606–610 Walnut Street. The store was wildly successful and took up three sections of the building it was in, rising to prominence in Muncie. Then fire struck after dark on November 26, 1924, causing an estimated $35,000 in damage— roughly 50 percent of the store's stock, primarily women's garments. The building itself was owned by Charles Indorf but suffered very little damage.

The fire, of unknown origin, started in the tailor shop. Wertheimer had been in the store with his wife only twenty minutes before the fire started and they were in a nearby theater when alerted of the blaze. Firefighters were quick and, despite the lack of daylight, were able to get five hoses and quench the flames in about an hour.

The fire revealed a secret behind the Hub's walls: the store was being used to "fence" stolen goods from other stores in the region. Prosecutor Van Louis Ogle was named receiver of the store and the corporation's holdings for the duration of the ongoing investigation. Receivership is a court-ordered situation where a business or estate is "placed in the custodial responsibility for the property of others, including tangible and intangible assets and rights." This is common during bankruptcies but also occurs when there is suspicion of impropriety. A union suspected of Mafia influence, for example, could temporarily be put under a receiver.

Following positive identification by manager Hilbert Larken Kain of clothing that had been stolen from an Albany store, authorities ordered the arrest of Lionel Wertheimer and Irvin Goldberg. They were held on $6,000 bond each. By December 8, several store owners from Indiana and Ohio had arrived to look over the Hub's inventory and identify items that had been taken in a string of nighttime burglaries. It was probably no coincidence that the Albany store was later torched by arson.

One Lucinda Goldberg testified before a grand jury, as did another store vice president, attorney Harvey Teed Bassett of Detroit, but neither was suspected of direct involvement in the crimes. Business records disclosed that the firm's incorporators included Bassett, Alma (Mrs. Lionel) Wertheimer of Muncie and Mert Wertheimer of Detroit—brother of Lionel and the subject of this chapter. Early on, the investigation pointed to Charles "One Arm" Wolf as a prime suspect in some of the burglaries, and he was picked up from a home on East Gilbert Street. Not coincidentally, Wolf was reported to be Goldberg's brother-in-law, though I could not confirm this. Another suspect was Earl Sheets of Muncie, not otherwise identified.

VAN L. OGLE

Prosecutor Van Ogle was the receiver for the Hub department store and later also convinced a jury to convict Charles Wolf on a murder charge. *From the Muncie Evening Press.*

Goldberg and Wertheimer posted bond but were immediately rearrested and brought to another county where one of the burglaries occurred. The number of charges against them continued to grow. The sheriff petitioned Governor Emmett Branch to extradite Harvey Bassett and Mert Wertheimer from Michigan for questioning and possible charges. Bassett had already appeared for questioning once, but the situation was evolving rapidly, and it now appeared he may not have been as forthcoming the first time as he could have been.

On December 12, Bassett and Mert Wertheimer were arrested on a conspiracy charge accusing them of being involved with Lionel Wertheimer, Goldberg and Wolf. The two men were released the same day when it was found there was no warrant to hold them. They vowed to fight extradition even if a warrant did arrive. Coming forward to defend the accused was attorney Maxwell Benjamin of Detroit, who said authorities were using their "usual" intimidation tactics on a corporation where "two of its employees have been suspected of a criminal offense." (Benjamin did not elaborate on what he meant by these "usual" tactics.) Benjamin, along with Muncie attorney Albert Elworth Needham, asked the court to set aside the receivership while the matter was being investigated. They said the Hub store was not insolvent or at risk of being insolvent, and while Ogle had the books, the store remained closed—an undue financial burden for the accused. Attorney Benjamin, incidentally, was the Mertheimer brothers' stepfather.

MAXWELL BENJAMIN

Maxwell Benjamin, a highly skilled Michigan attorney who also happened to be stepfather to the Wertheimer boys. *From the* Detroit Free Press.

While justice moved slowly in Muncie, it soldiered on in Detroit. On June 9, 1925, police under the command of Lieutenant William Hayes raided 113 State again, scooping up several blackjack players and dice throwers at the craps table. A total of thirty-three men were rounded up. The gambling den had only grown since the first raid, now often running all night and expanding its floor space, even using the next level of the building. The newspaper said the main room was lined with steel, with holes for riflemen to poke their weapons through. This was to prevent any hijackings by "thugs" as had happened at another gambling den in the recent past. The big stakes game was behind a heavy curtain for privacy. Wertheimer employed several bouncers, whom the press called "bruisers," to prevent trouble. An extra level of security came from a barbershop on the first floor. If police were seen entering the building, the barber pushed a button and lights flashed on the fourth floor where Wertheimer was. This would give his men enough time to scoop up any light items (dice and cash) and put them in a safe away from prying eyes. A craps table might still face the police hatchet, but the risk was reduced.

The continued operation of the club was brazen, to say the least. Rather than shut down or at least move locations, Wertheimer tried another tactic: he put the pool hall under the umbrella of the newly created Grand River Athletic Club, ostensibly a private organization for local boxers. However, authorities found that boxing was only a minimal part of the business. This was not a complete ruse, though: the club did have a boxing ring, a punching bag, bleachers for visitors and a rowing machine. Professional boxers did, in fact, train there on occasion. There was even a barber's chair and a shower stall for the athletes to clean up after.

Another Wertheimer brother, Alfred John Wertheimer, was also in the family business, running his own operation (the Park Avenue Health Club) out of the Charlevoix Hotel and facing constant police pressure. In fact, some sources suggest Al had been in the gambling game even longer than his older brother. According to news sources at the time, the Charlevoix catered to a classier clientele, while 113 State was for the more degenerate gamblers. Al caved in to police pressure and ceased gambling—at least as far as the police knew—in the summer of 1925.

At the end of June, 113 State was raided yet again, a mere two weeks after the last time. Lieutenant George Ludwig and his men smashed their way in, rounding up another twenty-five gamblers and charging them with being inmates of a gambling house. Gambling paraphernalia was again seized.

Around October 1, 1925, a trial against Goldberg and Lionel Wertheimer for receiving stolen property wrapped up, and the jury spent twelve hours deliberating before returning with a guilty verdict. The trial itself, before Judge Clarence Wilbur Dearth, lasted only two days and was very straightforward. The defense argued that the solen clothing was "planted" and the two men had never seen it before, which was not consistent with the facts. Because of the value of the clothing involved, the charges were akin to grand larceny, with both men facing fourteen years in state prison. They were given thirty days to appeal.

Using the court delays to his advantage, Lionel moved from Muncie to Palm Beach in 1925, where he went into the restaurant business. For more on the figure of Charles "One Arm" Wolf, readers should turn to the appendix.

Again and again, the men running gambling dens in Detroit were given slaps on the wrist, often because the laws were simply inadequate to do much more. They treated every time they were "shut down" as a mere pause before going full force once more. Prosecutor Eugene A. Walling intended to change all that in January 1926 when he filed an injunction to get five of Detroit's most notorious places padlocked and their belongings sold. In addition, the owners would be further barred from operating in Wayne County (greater Detroit) ever again. In addition to Wertheimer's Grand River Athletic Club, Walling targeted the Berghoff Grill (54 Monroe Street), Charles "Doc" Brady, John Ryan and Charles Clark. Brady was second only to Wertheimer in his press coverage and defiance of the police.

The kidnapping in March 1926 of Meyer "Fish" Bloomfield, a stickman at Doc Brady's casino, kicked off a wave of snatchings blamed on New York gunmen. Brady paid $40,000 or more for the return of his employee. This was the first of a long series of kidnappings of gambling house operators for ransom. Over the next year, Brady himself would be ransomed for $35,000, and Lefty Clark (alias William Bischoff) brought in $40,000, John Ryan $50,000, Ruby Mathis $25,000, Louis Rosenbaum $15,000, Abraham Fein $14,000, Joe Klein $10,000 and Dick Driscoll $20,000. These cases were all handled internally and only reached the press through rumor and gossip.

Wertheimer was held at one point for $30,000 and later admitted as much publicly. He was taken along with a "henchman" to a summer cottage outside Chicago. The other man was brought back to Detroit to secure payment. Lou Wertheimer was brought to a window and shown his brother being held in a taxicab and allegedly told the kidnappers, "Have him run up and down on the sidewalk so I can see if his arms and legs are okay. I don't pay for damaged merchandise."

The death knell of 113 State appeared to ring on April 9, 1927, when police took out Wertheimer's safe and brought it back to the station for inspection. The writer who reported on the story for the *Detroit Free Press* was given no byline, but I'll quote at length from his flowery prose marking the occasion. Wertheimer was a major adversary of the police, accused of being a dealer "in ivory, pasteboard and cupidity." His safe brought everyone on the force to the scene. "If you have never seen 100 policemen all agog, and what a sight it is, you should have begged sick and dropped in at headquarters." The police could not open the safe, so volunteer civilians brought "files and hammers and chisels and muscles." Each one failed. One man shouted out that the safe probably had $50,000 in it, and another shouted back it likely had double that amount.

George Wilson of the Diebold Safe Company was called in. He was an expert with his stethoscope and could hear the tumblers fall into place. Yet even Wilson found it a challenge: sweat was visible on his face. "Toughest job I ever had," he told the crowd. "They musta put the mint in here." After the final click, Wilson called out, "Hot dog!" The safe opened to reveal "a very dead angleworm" and "a splintered piece of broom handle." The police wondered "whether the broom handle was used to slay the angleworm, or whether the angleworm broke the broom." This was their "most crushing disappointment…since horse cars crept along Woodward Avenue." Judge William Brown formally ordered 113 State padlocked on June 30, 1927, banning it from operation for one year.

On March 12, 1929, Al Wertheimer was picked up at his gambling joint, the Aniwa Club at East Jefferson and VanDyke, by Detroit police commissioner William Rutledge. Also brought in were entertainers Charles Adler and Oscar Herman. The reason was not gambling: police suspected Wertheimer knew something of the St. Valentine's Day Massacre in Chicago. In fact, Al acknowledged he was acquainted with two of the men police said were suspects but swore he did not know them on a personal level. One month later, Detroit mayor John Christian Lodge blasted Rutledge when it was revealed he had a personal connection to the Aniwa Club and had not shut down the club as ordered. The establishment did not last long after that. (Lodge, incidentally, was an uncle of aviator Charles Lindbergh.) Al Wertheimer next opened the Shawnee Club in Cleveland, which tried to evade police by hiding roulette tables under ping-pong games. Chief George Matowitz of Cleveland was less forgiving than Rutledge and shuttered the place as soon as possible.

The newspapers and radio frequently took the side of the law against gamblers and corrupt politicians. Jerry Buckley, a WMBC radio man with a program on Detroit civics, was an outspoken critic of graft in the Detroit area, not afraid to mention Wertheimer and his friends by name. Buckley was fiercely opposed to pro-gambling Mayor Charles Bowles, and many credited Buckley with getting the mayor recalled. In July 1930, Buckley was shot and killed in the lobby of the LaSalle Hotel, which housed WMBC. Newspaper editorials praised his bravery and blasted Detroit for being a haven for Chicago and New York gangsters. The *Binghamton Press*, for example, believed it was likely Buckley's killers were brought in from out of town for the job, aided by local men who were greasing the pockets of politicians and police.

This nondescript building housed an early Wertheimer gambling venture known as the Aniwa Club. *Author collection.*

The free press opposed to the underworld only became more vociferous when one of their own was killed, and media pressure increased.

Following what appeared to be a successful campaign against gambling in Detroit, a number of big-time operators spilled over into Toronto and set up shop there. Underworld rumors were that it was harder to "grease the bulls" (bribe police) in Canada, and profits were smaller, but if you stayed quiet, there was enough money going around to get by. Some men were not very good at staying quiet. William Pheltemate, colorfully nicknamed "Whitey the Pest," tried to set up shop at the King Edward Hotel and found himself in a fistfight with hotel detectives.

With gambling under attack in Detroit and Wertheimer one of several men targeted by kidnappers, he tried to reinvent himself in Miami Beach. By 1932, he was the managing director of the Beach and Tennis Club on Lincoln Road near the ocean, in the mansion formerly owned by automotive entrepreneur Carl Graham Fisher. This was an upstanding resort, by all appearances, with world-class entertainment. An early celebrity performer was Ziegfeld Follies singer-actress Helen Morgan. In Miami Beach, Wertheimer was publicly transformed from underworld figure to respected citizen. On one occasion in 1935, he rubbed elbows with actor George Bancroft as they presided over the Miss Miami Beach contest—which also had prizes for Miss Seminole Indian and Most Perfect Baby. Wertheimer, alongside colleague Deane Thompson, was continually celebrated in the press for his Beach and Tennis Club's hospitality. Later reports would even say Mert had "sponsored" the "first Orange Bowl game," but this has proven very difficult to corroborate.

The federal government cracked down hard on Wertheimer's Detroit friends in March 1936, using what they said was the same law that crippled Al Capone. Warrants for tax evasion for the years 1929 to 1930 came down against Sullivan, Fitzgerald, George Weinbrenner and five lesser-known gamblers (John Grace, Thomas Gleason, Samuel Myers, Cornelius Hurley and Frank Licini). Prosecuting attorney Gregory Frederick said that during those years, these three operated a gambling den at 17100 Mack Avenue. Frederick said as of the indictment, they were still running an illegal casino at the Chesterfield Inn on Gratior Avenue. The three men allegedly owed $181,187 in taxes, not including what the other five men owed.

January 1937 brought the moment that Wertheimer was launched from local to national fame when he claimed to have found a loophole in Florida's gambling laws at the Royal Palm Club he managed for Miami alderman Arthur Childers. Although gambling devices such as slot machines and roulette tables were illegal, the state did offer a chance to license "other devices" that operated by coin for $1,000 each. When slot machines were registered as "other" coin-operated devices, they were then, in theory, under the protection of the state. Dice and roulette balls were dispensed to patrons from a vending machine for fifty cents each, thus making them also part of the "coin-operated devices" category. Because the patron was able to keep the ball or dice after they were done using them, their purchase was of the objects and not the gambling itself. Wertheimer's role in the Royal Palm brought the club unwanted attention, with columnists like Jack Bell openly calling him a "front man" for underworld figures.

State attorney George Ambrose Worley and county solicitor Robert Rives Taylor strongly objected to this use of the licensing law. They said there was no way the 1935 law was intended to protect slot machines and other gambling devices in this way. However, they declined to conduct any raids or prosecute until further research was done and a firm answer came down from the attorney general. Whether Wertheimer was correct or not, he had

Although it had been closed for many years by this time, the legendary Chesterfield Inn ended in a raging fire for countless onlookers. *From the* Detroit Free Press.

effectively held law enforcement off and had eight machines legally licensed through the end of October, when the annual license would expire. He further informed the authorities that gambling would only be permitted for non-Florida residents, though it's unclear why that mattered.

Attorney General Cary Dayton Landis decided that Wertheimer had beat the system and would be allowed to operate. New licenses would not be permitted, but this gave Wertheimer a virtual monopoly—his eight licenses were the only ones given a blessing by the state.

In January 1939, the Wertheimers' stepfather Maxwell Benjamin started his new career as an assistant attorney general in Michigan. Less than one hour later, he was fired by newly elected Attorney General Thomas Read when Read learned of the family connection. Read told the press,

> *They can't do this to me. This office is going to be clean. I won't stand for anything questionable. The man goes off the payroll immediately....I have a high regard for Mr. Benjamin's legal ability and a high regard for his character. I think he is a very fine gentleman and would render the state a very splendid service, but it has been brought to my attention that Mr. Benjamin is the stepfather of the Wertheimer boys, and inasmuch as the*

27

gambling question is prominently in the public eye, it seems inadvisable for this department to have Mr. Benjamin associated with the office. I regret very much having to do this, and I feel personally that Mr. Benjamin has no connection either directly or indirectly with the gambling interests of this state. In fact, I am sure that Mr. Benjamin personally is a lawyer whose character and reputation are above reproach. Mr. Benjamin has not been associated with this office and will not be associated with this office. The matter is closed.

Read would not say who had recommended Benjamin for the position but said, "I don't know any of the Wertheimers. I never talked to any of them. I had no idea Benjamin was related to them." The only thing Read would comment publicly about the hiring was that he thought it would be wise to add a Jewish man to his office and Benjamin came highly recommended by Jewish organizations in Detroit. Assistant attorney general Willard McIntyre favored Benjamin because he was from a small town (Cheboygan) and thought this would be a benefit. It's not clear exactly how McIntyre meant this, but perhaps a small town-man would more likely appear "clean."

Benjamin had been a practicing attorney in Detroit for thirty-eight years, preceding any association with the Wertheimer brothers. He was highly respected and was a thirty-second-degree Mason, schmoozing with many influential men in business and politics. However, Read had recently been directed by Governor Frank Fitzgerald to look into gambling in Macomb County (Detroit's northern suburbs), and the timing of his hiring rubbed many people the wrong way. When Fitzgerald was asked about the hiring and firing, he declined to comment beyond saying, "I think Tom did right." When contacted by the press, Benjamin acknowledged his family link:

Yes, they're my stepsons. I can't deny it and I have no wish to. I have no connection with the gambling business, however. I married Mrs. Wertheimer in 1907 and helped bring the boys up....If you've ever met them, you'll agree they are fine gentlemen. I do not condone their business and have no part or connection with it. You'll agree Mert is tops in his profession, however. He knows some of the biggest men in the country. He is known all over the United States as a clean gambler. If he weren't honest and upright, he couldn't have made the success he has made.

By sheer coincidence, Governor Fitzgerald died in office a mere two months later, age fifty-four.

At the same time as the Benjamin firing, the East Detroit Civic League was granted an injunction against the Chesterfield Inn, an alleged gambling den on Gratiot Avenue in East Detroit (today known as Eastpointe). The press reported that "droves" of "well-dressed patrons" were forced from the premises, and more were turned away as they approached the parking lot. The operators were identified as Lincoln Fitzgerald (no relation to the governor), Danny Sullivan and Mert Wertheimer. However, with his primary residence being in Florida, Wertheimer likely had little hands-on involvement. Fitzgerald had been active in gambling in Macomb and Wayne Counties since the early 1920s but, despite his notoriety, remained largely untouched by the law. Sullivan likewise had a long history with gambling but only really made headlines in 1936 when the government claimed he owed $463,000 in back taxes (roughly $10.2 million in today's dollars). He settled the debt for $237,000 and avoided any jail time.

Inside the shuttered Chesterfield was found a sign consisting of rules for employees. They were told to get plenty of rest and arrive to their shifts early. The dress code required shined shoes, a handkerchief, a black bowtie, a white shirt and white suspenders. Despite this being a casino, employees were not allowed to gamble at the Chesterfield or anywhere else. Above all, employees must be clean: "Take at least three baths weekly."

On March 10, 1939, Florida attorney general George Couper Gibbs, aided by Governor Frederick Cone, made his move to halt gambling. Five ministers sought and received an injunction against the Plantation casino, naming ten operators of the business. Along with Wertheimer was another Detroit gangster, "John Doe" Bernstein. The ministers alleged in their complaint that the Plantation ran bingo games with prizes as high as $2,500 and had no fewer than seventeen roulette wheels in operation, eight craps tables and more.

On July 22, 1943, the St. Clair Shores Methodist Men's Club wrote to Governor Harry Kelly, demanding he remove Sheriff Jacob Frank Theut from office in Macomb County. They further requested the governor send in the state police, as they believed local officials were accepting bribes in exchange for allowing gambling to flourish. The letter came on the heels of allegations that slot machines were present at the Jefferson Beach Amusement Park, as well as a resort across the street from the park. The primary owner of these establishments was John Zeno "Mike" Brunton, but other owners included Mert Wertheimer and Danny Sullivan. Press reports alleged the deal was brokered by no less a person than a former Macomb prosecutor.

Sheriff Theut defended himself publicly, saying,

They have a 12-man police force there in St. Clair Shores. I have but 15 men to police the entire county. As a result I have been plenty busy outside the incorporated areas. However, now that I find St. Clair Shores officers cannot be relied upon to handle their own problem, I have stepped in. In the future, gambling just won't exist there. I'll take care of that personally.

The press looked into the matter and found that the slot machines had been removed within a matter of days but also noticed three of Theut's fifteen men directing traffic near Jefferson Beach's parking lot. The conclusion they drew was this: the sheriff had no interest in shutting down Wertheimer, Sullivan and Fitzgerald. He was happy to look the other way if things remained hidden.

On August 1, 1946, a Macomb County one-man grand jury under the authority of Judge Herman Dehnke brought down indictments against the local gambling element. Charging them with gambling violations and obstruction of justice, Dehnke named Wertheimer, Sullivan and Fitzgerald, as well as William Henry McKeighan, a former mayor of Flint and political ally of Republican machine boss Frank McKay. McKeighan had a long history of alleged corruption, resulting in numerous court appearances: stuffing ballot boxes in 1928 (acquitted); Prohibition violations in 1932 (acquitted); accepting a $500,000 bribe along with Frank McKay in 1940 (mistrial, with rumored jury tampering); retried on the same charges in 1942 (acquitted); and taking $200,000 in bribes with McKay in 1945 (acquitted). This last charge resulted from a grand jury probe run by state senator Kimber Cornellus "Kim" Sigler, who, to his credit, was from the same political party as McKeighan and McKay.

Dehnke also named several unindicted coconspirators: slot machine king Arthur Peter Sauve, deputy sheriff Lewis Burt, state senator Ivan Johnston (already on trial for perjury), prosecutor Wilbur Held (recently forced to resign), police captain Laurence Lyon (already serving thirty days for contempt) and police sergeant Leslie Vern Maycock. Johnston would later face more perjury charges when he switched back and forth between "knowing" a man named Manny Barg and "never meeting him" multiple times in a single grilling under oath. Gambling establishments identified were Jefferson Beach, Marjo's, Eastwood Park, Club Royale and the Kopper Kettle. Dehnke told the press, "This is just the beginning. There is much more to be done. So far we have just scratched the surface."

He authorized Captain Donald Leonard of the state police to bring in the indicted men.

Senator Johnston, perhaps not coincidentally, was a critic of the Sigler grand jury that indicted McKeighan. He chaired a committee to investigate Sigler's expenditures. A verbal battle between the two broke out, resulting in Johnston suing Sigler for libel, without success. Johnston lost reelection and fell from grace, while Sigler's star was on the rise and saw him nominated for governor (and winning).

Warrants were issued by Dehnke, though there was a small hurdle: Sullivan and Fitzgerald were believed to be in Las Vegas, while Wertheimer and McKeighan were in Miami. McKeighan was thought to have pivoted away from gambling and toward the Florida hotel industry. Though Wertheimer may have been a "gangster" in Detroit, he was respected in Florida. Shortly before the indictment came down, columnist Jimmy Powers wrote glowingly that "Mert Wertheimer runs the swankiest of all casinos at the Colonial Inn. He pays his girls $150 a week but they need it to live on because of the inflationary prices." Reporter Robert Lodmell said the Colonial Inn was estimated to have made $3 million from gambling in the previous year, with the next one expected to bring more. When Florida authorities went looking to serve the Michigan warrants, they found McKeighan in Miami Beach, though he vowed to fight extradition. Wertheimer could not be found and was widely suspected of being in Cuba, outside the long arm of the law. Cuba was a popular gambler hangout in the pre-Castro era. Broward County authorities said they were not surprised Wertheimer was not around; his club was closed for the season, so he had no reason to be on-site.

Local newspapers in Michigan praised Dehnke's one-man crusade. One editorial the day after the indictments said,

> *For the first time in the history of Macomb County law enforcement (which until the present has had no very bright chapters) warrants have been issued against key malefactors. Charged with conspiracy to violate gaming laws and obstruct justice are Mert Wertheimer, Danny Sullivan and Lincoln Fitzgerald. So notorious are these three in the realm of professional gambling that their names stand as synonyms for corruption—because the scale on which they conducted gaming places is impossible unless politicians and policemen have been bought.*

In mid-August, while the grand jury's work continued, "slot machine king" Arthur Sauve was under guard by the state police because he was considered

COLONIAL INN

Above: The "swanky" Colonial Inn, a popular gambling resort for those vacationing in Florida. *From the* Miami Herald.

Left: An ad for the Colonial Inn showing this wasn't an underground club but very much a celebrated part of nightlife. *From the* Miami Herald.

Star Spangled Preview!

Mert Wertheimer's

COLONIAL INN

(Federal highway No. 1 at Hallandale)

Opening Informally
Thursday, December 27

Harry Richman

(with Sid Franklin at piano)

Mary Ray & Naldi

Dick Gasparre's
Orchestra

Reservations
Telephone Hollywood 1054-1055

the "ace witness" of the case. Sauve had testified that McKeighan was the payoff man to enable gambling in Macomb County: gambling dens would pay McKeighan, who passed on bribes to the police. Sauve said Danny Sullivan explained that McKeighan was "not exactly a partner" in the gambling business but "handled lots of business dealings for them." Sauve himself received $1,100 each month to be passed on to Captain Laurence Lyon and Sergeant Maycock. Judge Dehnke wanted Sauve protected at all costs, pointing to the murder of state senator Warren Hooper, who had been murdered during a prior graft investigation in 1945. Dehnke also instructed the state police to suspend Sergeant William Hedt from his post at Mount Pleasant. Hedt had been appearing before the grand jury "almost daily," and Dehnke did not like what he was hearing. The sergeant had been on the force since 1920, but charges were pending based on the time he was stationed in Detroit from 1940 to 1945.

McKeighan had been arrested in Florida by September 8, but he fought his extradition, claiming he had never "in any way been a partner with the three men indicted with me." Dehnke filed several documents consisting of affidavits alleging that McKeighan was the "payoff man," including one by a newly revealed bribery target: Macomb County sheriff Robert Havel, who held the position from 1937 to 1940. Havel said McKeighan had given him a total of $15,000 from campaign contributions over the years, particularly during election season—whether he ended up winning or not.

At the end of September 1946, Judge Dehnke released a second indictment charging four policemen with accepting bribes to allow gambling and four other men with maintaining slot machines at the Arethusa Hotel in Mount Clemens. The police officers were state police captain Laurence Lyon, Sergeant Leslie Maycock, Sergeant William Hedt and Sergeant Stanley Carlson. The Arethusa men were Arthur Sauve, ex-boxer John Achiel Sierens, Herman Elwood Hodnett and Morris Feldman. Appearing in court on October 3, all eight men pleaded guilty. Other than Lyon and Sauve, the men were allowed to go free while awaiting sentencing. Two members of the "Polish Bank" mutuel house (floating gambling operation), Joseph Pawloski and Frank Nadolpski, were fined $250 each for "false and evasive answers to the grand jury."

Around October 10, Mert Wertheimer showed up in Macomb County with attorney Louis Colombo to be served his warrant. He flew in to Willow Run Airport (just outside Detroit) from Chicago. Wertheimer was released on $2,500 bond that was furnished by bondsman Abe Hertzberg, and a hearing was set for October 30. Wertheimer appeared in good spirits and told the press, "I wasn't hiding. I don't know why nobody could find me." He did concede he was "all over the country," which might have made the search difficult. When asked why he showed up in Macomb rather than fight extradition, he said matter-of-factly, "I just decided to come back, that's all."

Between Wertheimer's being served and his first hearing, Raymond "Ruby" Mathis was indicted for running the Kopper Kettle gambling establishment in Macomb County. Like his gambling friends, Mathis had been bouncing around Florida and Reno before voluntarily surrendering on October 23. Another $2,500 bond was posted by Abe Hertzberg. In addition to Mathis's ties to Wertheimer, Dehnke introduced a name new to readers in his charges: Sol Adaskin, said to be a partner in the Kopper Kettle. Attorney Louis Colombo entered a guilty plea for Mathis, who faced up to two years in prison. At the same time, Colombo informed Dehnke that he would not be able to attend Wertheimer's next hearing, causing the judge to push it off to an indefinite date.

The trial against Ivan Johnston began on April 11, 1947, with a strong opening statement from prosecutor Melvin Orr. Johnston was accused of accepting bribes from gamblers and houses of prostitution in 1938, during his campaign for Macomb County district attorney, in exchange for favors while he was office (1939–42). In addition, Johnston allegedly pressured Wilbur Held to drop out of the same race in exchange for a promise to be appointed Johnston's chief assistant. Once elected, Johnston continued to accept bribes from bookie John Sierens and brothel operator Benson McGlynn, among others. McGlynn's operation on the outskirts of Mount Clemens was known as the Oaks and was considered "swanky" by the local press. Further, Johnston allegedly directed deputy sheriff Lewis Burt to collect from two other brothels and the head of the Polish Bank numbers syndicate. Orr explained to the jury, "We will show he even arranged collections from a once-a-week bingo game at the Maple Lane Golf Club."

The first witness against Johnston was Lewis Burt, who laid out the collections he was personally involved in. He took money from brothel operators "Jean" and "Whitey" at various establishments, Polish Bank operators Leo "Dick" Walsh and Jack Teasdale, Bert Ramler at Maple Lane Golf Club and Art Sully, who ran a bingo game at Harper and 10 Mile. Burt collected $225 from McGlynn at the Oaks four times, with $200 going directly to Johnston. After the fourth time, the state police raided the brothel, and following that, it burned down. Otherwise, collections would have continued.

Wilbur Held, assistant under Johnston, was a reluctant witness during his four days on the stand, but he made various admissions when faced with transcripts of earlier testimony he gave before Judge Dehnke behind closed doors. Held specifically made the direct connection between the Wertheimer gambling syndicate and Johnston. Although this was secondhand information, Held explained how Johnston told him that each month he would meet McKeighan in a Detroit hotel room and accept $1,500, which was a lump payment from the various gambling houses. Such payments began in early 1939 when Johnston first took office and continued as long as gambling houses were up and running.

Wertheimer was finally arraigned in June 1947 and entered in a plea of not guilty. Judge Chester Palmer O'Hara continued his bond. The delays were likely due in part to his three codefendants all fighting extradition, but O'Hara vowed to bring Wertheimer to trial in the near future. In fact, the trial did come quickly and went out with a whimper. Through a plea deal in early July, Wertheimer was found guilty of gambling, while charges of obstructing justice and bribery were tossed out. He was ordered to pay a fine of $2,500 plus $4,000 in costs but served no jail time. Prosecutor Melvin Orr was pleased with Wertheimer's "voluntary appearance and cooperation."

Editorials wondered if this was what justice looked like and sarcastically praised "good old Mert." How nice of him to be cooperative and thus avoid the jail time that likely would have come with a bribery conviction. As one editor wrote,

A prison sentence, it seems, would not be good sportsmanship when Mert had been so darned obliging about the whole matter. We confess bafflement at the logic of our law as interpreted at Mt. Clemens, but that, of course, has nothing to do with good old Mert. Here's hoping that in coming out in his new joint he never throws anything but sevens or elevens!

On July 24, 1947, Max Kerner began a thirty-day jail sentence for contempt of court. Kerner, part owner of the Jefferson Beach Amusement Park, had not cooperated with the grand jury investigating gambling and frequently claimed to have "lapses of memory." Judge Dehnke did not find this convincing as a way to explain his "evasive, false and contradictory statements." Kerner's silence was widely seen as protecting Wertheimer.

With Sullivan and Fitzgerald still wanted in Michigan, Nevada began to acquire a reputation as an asylum for gamblers. "The integrity and honesty of Nevada is at stake because of these continued delays in the carrying out of justice," Attorney General Alan Bible said during the Fitzgerald and Sullivan case on September 30, 1947. Even with gambling legal in Nevada, they had no authority to protect citizens from the laws of other states.

On January 27, 1948, Danny Sullivan and Lincoln Fitzgerald, now operators of the Nevada Club at 224 North Virginia Street in Reno, were held in the Washoe County jail while awaiting extradition. They were ordered held by Judge William Davidson Hatton of Tonopah after a writ of habeas corpus was denied, based on directions from Nevada governor Vail Montgomery Pittman. The pair announced their intention to appeal, and Attorney General Bible requested they be held without bail pending any appeal. On their booking cards, both men listed their residence as the Riverside Hotel, LaVere Redfield's favorite casino. They had working for them a team of three criminal attorneys: William Cashill, C.E. Horton and W. Howard Gray.

Due to complaints about Fitzgerald's and Sullivan's constitutional rights being denied, the matter also went federal. In February, federal judge Roger Thomas Foley ruled the same as Tonopah district judge Hatton had: that Michigan's affidavit was adequate, Fitzgerald and Sullivan were fugitives and the extradition documents met the legal requirements. He granted them each bail of $5,000. Attorney Cashill appealed to the federal circuit court of appeals in San Francisco. Months passed while awaiting a court date.

On March 24, Fitzgerald and Sullivan were still awaiting extradition, while more affidavits were being prepared to smooth over any objections. Arthur Sauve appeared before U.S. Commissioner George Reed and swore that he met the pair, along with Mert Wertheimer, in a Detroit hotel room. "Mert wanted to know if I could take care of Captain Laurence Lyon and Sergeant Leslie Maycock." Following this meeting, he passed on $800 to Lyon and $300 to Maycock, both on a monthly basis, so "they wouldn't be knocking off the joints."

In August, the Macomb County sheriff, C. Scott Burke, and prosecutor Edward Jacob clandestinely traveled to Reno, where their movements and dealings were kept secret. Finally, on August 11, the fight was over and the Nevada gamblers were in Detroit for arraignment. Sullivan and Fitz voluntarily surrendered the day before and flew to Michigan with Jacob and Burke. They waived their right to a preliminary hearing and were released on $2,500 bond each while awaiting trial. Switching their pleas to guilty, the men walked out of Judge James Eldredge Spier's court days later after paying fines and costs totaling $52,000. Though the charges against them could have resulted in jail time, they were merely told to keep their noses clean and stay out of the state—something they had been trying to do anyway. A lesser-known member of their syndicate, the aforementioned John "Mike" Brunton, was brought to court around the same time with similar results.

Mert's brother Lionel Wertheimer, commonly known as Wert, passed away in September 1948 at age fifty-seven. His premature death was a shock to family and friends, as he went from healthy to sick in a matter of hours. An emergency surgery was ordered but was ultimately unsuccessful. Though Lionel had once been associated with Mert in the Hub store and all the problems that came with it, he had dramatically improved his station, without the taint of his three brothers. At the time of his passing, Lionel was a celebrated restaurateur in Palm Beach, Florida, affectionately called "colorful" by the local press. He operated Wert's at 456 South Ocean Boulevard. Although the building no longer stands, the property sold for $26 million in 2021, to give you an idea of how coveted this location was. So respected was Lionel in Palm Beach that one of his pallbearers was no less than local police chief Eddie Longo.

On December 22, 1948, former prosecutor Wilbur Held was convicted of accepting bribes and obstruction of justice. The star witness was Arthur Sauve, who spoke of passing on $3,600 to buy a "liberal attitude" toward slot machines. Held was given time to file motions before a sentence was handed down by Judge Joseph Sanford, and Held's attorney Harrison Watson vowed to appeal to the state supreme court. Watson had argued that Held was granted immunity related to his dealings with Wertheimer, Fitzgerald and Sullivan and that Sauve was an agent of these men, not a separate case.

In April 1949, leaving Detroit and Florida behind, Mert applied for city licenses to operate blackjack, craps, roulette and slot machines at the Riverside Hotel in Reno. At this point, his brother Lou was better known in town because he had the gambling license for the Mapes Hotel, which was across the street. Lou, described as "suave" and a "sharp dresser," was partners with horse fixer Bernie Einstoss and Charlie Mapes. The Mapes Hotel, for many years, was the tallest building in Nevada, a title it would hold until 1956. Mert's application was approved, and gambling at the Riverside was transferred to him from famed gambling pioneer Nathan "Nick" Abelman, who had taken up ownership of the nearby Waldorf Club when the prior owner, Howard Farris, defaulted on a loan from Abelman. Wertheimer establishing himself in Nevada seems like a natural progression of his talents and the sign of a mature man no longer wanting the stress of evading the law. However, this did not keep newspaper editors from speculating that Mert did not move to Reno by choice but rather was pushed out of Florida by some "friendly muscle" from the mob operating in Broward County.

Did Mert bring some trouble with him to Reno? By November 1949, Lincoln Fitzgerald and his wife, Meta, had moved to a new house on Mark Twain Avenue in southwest Reno, but someone had apparently been following Fitz for a while. Around midnight on November 19, as he was stepping outside to go to the club, a gunman emerged from the bushes and fired multiple shots from a double-barreled shotgun into Fitz's back at close range—so close, in fact, that some of the wadding from a charge became embedded in Fitzgerald's back. Meta ran out to see him flailing and told her husband, "Quit moving your arms!" He then lay still until the ambulance arrived.

The ambulance had been alerted by Fitzgerald's neighbor, Joseph F. McDonald, who happened to be the editor of the *Nevada State Journal*. McDonald reported firsthand the next morning,

> *I had just gone to bed about a quarter to midnight when I heard two shots right together. "Whang, whang." It sounded like somebody had a cannon. I ran downstairs in my pajamas and went out the back door, crossing the yard to the fence next to the Fitzgerald home where I heard a woman screaming. I asked "What's happened?" and Mrs. Fitzgerald said "Somebody's been shot." I ran back into the house to call the police and an ambulance and put on a robe.*

At the Washoe Medical Center, Fitzgerald was questioned by Chief Lorenz Russell Greeson. He denied knowing who shot him and would not say if the shooter had come from Detroit because of an old feud. That Fitzgerald could speak at all was a miracle, as he had 110 shotgun pellets in him and doctors said his chances of survival were "very, very slim." His spine appeared to be severed, causing paralysis below the waist. Aside from that, Fitzgerald, who did not smoke or drink, was in good health, and he did his best to rally as transfusions kept him alive. Police told the press that robbery was not suspected as a motive. Detective Michael Salonisen noted that not a single dollar was taken from Fitzgerald and explained, "It couldn't have been robbery. It must have been revenge." Greeson was asked by the press if the shooter was a member of Detroit's Purple Gang. He doubted this, saying that "the gang occasionally hung out at" places run by Fitzgerald but there was "no direct tieup."

With Fitzgerald not talking, the police turned to his friend Sullivan, who said, "In this work, you never know who hates you. The way they are snatching babies and killing children these days, you never can tell what might happen." Sullivan did say he knew of no one specifically who would have a motive to hurt Fitzgerald. This did not stop newspapers from speculating. Reporter Wilson McGee noted that although gang violence was virtually unknown in Reno, this was the third time in the recent past that gunmen had targeted gamblers formerly associated with Broward County, Florida. John "Big Jack" Letendre (a former Rhode Island politician) was shot down in April 1946 after refusing to turn his gambling interests over to New York mobsters. More famously, Benjamin "Bugsy" Siegel was killed in Beverly Hills in June 1947; he previously had "a piece" of the Colonial Inn.

Through some miracle (or perhaps a gambler's luck), less than two days after the attack, feeling returned to Fitzgerald's feet. A doctor, speaking anonymously, said, "It is possible the spinal cord hasn't been as severely damaged as was feared. Some of the initial effect may have been concussion." To everyone's surprise, the patient showed "a lot of improvement," though it would be at least five more days before they could remove him from the critical list. Ultimately, Fitzgerald was released in early April 1950 (several months after the shooting) and was doing "fine." Newspapers spread the rumor that he would now live in a steel and concrete apartment built over the Nevada Club, but Danny Sullivan said this was hogwash. "Fitz can rest upstairs if he wants," Sullivan said, but the elevators going upstairs had a variety of uses and were not some secret entrance.

The summer of 1950 turned out to be a time of Congressional inquiry for Wertheimer. On July 3, a Senate banking subcommittee looked into a $975,000 loan from the Reconstruction Finance Corporation (RFC) to Lou Wertheimer and the Mapes Hotel. The RFC had been set up in 1932 to inject federal money into the economy but had come under increasing scrutiny since the end of the Great Depression and World War II (it was disbanded completely in 1957). An investigation centered on loan examiner Hilton Robertson for approving the loan over objections from the committee at large. Why did Robertson fund Wertheimer and his partners, Frank Grannis and horse race fixer Bernard Einstoss, both alleged to be close associates of Los Angeles gangster Mickey Cohen? Further, was it right for federal dollars to fund a hotel that made 98 percent of its profits from gambling and catered to couples seeking divorces? Robertson said he did not care who owned or operated the hotel. What they did in Reno was legal, and the bottom line was that it was a good investment.

Virgil Peterson, operating director of the Chicago Crime Commission, testified to the Kefauver Committee on July 7, 1950:

> *Another gambling syndicate operated in Michigan is known as the Chesterfield syndicate. It has been operated in Michigan. The head of the Chesterfield syndicate is Mert Wertheimer, who is one of the biggest gamblers in the entire nation. Wertheimer now has the gambling concession at a hotel in Reno, Nevada. Next to Wertheimer in importance in the Chesterfield syndicate was Lincoln Fitzgerald, who is now operating the Nevada Club, Reno, Nevada, with Daniel Sullivan, also from Michigan. Other members of the Chesterfield syndicate in Michigan have included Lefty Clark, Red Gorman, Mike Brunton, and Al Driscoll. Records recently recovered from Frank Erickson by the district attorney in New York definitely established that Wertheimer was a partner in the elaborate gambling casino known as the Colonial Inn, Hallandale, Florida, some time ago....The records reflected that Wertheimer was associated in the Colonial Inn with some of the most notorious gangsters in the country, including Joe Adonis, alias Joe Doto; Vincent Alo, alias Jimmy Blue Eyes; Meyer Lansky, Jake Lansky, and Frank Erickson, all of whom were members of the Frank Costello mob of New York.*

The records referred to by Peterson were made public in New York that May during the trial of Frank Erickson. Wertheimer was alleged to be part of Detroit's notorious Purple Gang and had a 32.5 percent stake in the Colonial Inn. This was by far the single biggest piece of the pie. According to prosecutors in the Erickson trial, Wertheimer made $222,800 from this establishment in a one-year period (1945–46) before it was shut down and converted to a burlesque house.

On November 14, 1950, the Kefauver hearings moved to Los Angeles. William J. Moore was up first. An architect by trade, he came to Las Vegas in 1941 to design the Hotel Last Frontier for his uncle, movie theater mogul R.E. Griffith, and operated the casino, which opened as the second major property on the Strip in October 1942, after his uncle's death. In addition to his duties at the Last Frontier, Moore served as a member of the Nevada Tax Commission, the administrative body that oversaw the collection of taxes from Nevada businesses, including casinos. Moore revealed that since the Tax Commission had begun issuing licenses, it had refused "hundreds" of applications and revoked as many as one hundred licenses for reasons of "character." Halley asked why William Graham and James McKay, notorious

Reno racketeers mentioned earlier, had been granted licenses despite their convictions for altering government bonds in the southern district of New York. They remained qualified, Moore insisted, because of a "granddaddy clause" that allowed those who were operating before the more stringent regulatory regime was adopted to continue to do so. Mert Wertheimer of Detroit was licensed after a testimonial from the "former head of the FBI from Detroit." Moore knew of Wertheimer's gambling activities in other states but insisted that shouldn't disqualify him. "The man gambles," he explained. "That is no sign he shouldn't have a license in a state where it is legal." This was a "basic policy" of the Tax Commission.

In February 1951, Wertheimer himself was subpoenaed to appear before the Kefauver Committee. U.S. Marshal Leonard Carpenter had charge of serving the papers and accomplished it without any complications. Carpenter told the press that, as far as he knew, no other Reno figures had been summoned by the committee. Al Klein, counsel for the committee, said a session would be held soon in San Francisco or Los Angeles and Wertheimer would not have to travel to Washington, D.C. When asked why Wertheimer was wanted, Klein said it was to answer questions about "the operation of his establishment" and "about his associates."

Kefauver committee counsel William Ruymann met with Wertheimer and the pair had a conversation. Ruymann told the press Wertheimer was "helpful and cooperative." He declined to reveal what was discussed. Ruymann also spoke with Charles Mapes. He sought but could not find Ruby Mathis, Lou Wertheimer and Bernard Einstoss.

Due in part to past controversies involving Wertheimer, Sullivan and Fitzgerald, the gambling division of the Nevada Tax Commission initiated two policies in May 1951: first, effective July 1951, no Nevada bookmaker or sports pool could accept bets on horse races or other sporting events from any out-of-state person or source, and second, as of January 1952, gambling licenses would be denied to any individual who owned or controlled gaming interests outside Nevada. Simply put, this would make sure gamblers were operating only where it was legal: in Nevada.

In August 1951, Lou Wertheimer left the Mapes Hotel and joined Mert and Ruby Mathis at the Riverside. By the time Lou joined them, LaVere Redfield was already a Riverside regular, with another occasional visitor being amateur musician Marie Michaud. By chance, the two became acquainted, and Redfield's wandering eye brought her into his orbit.

41

Chapter 3

THE DAME

M arie Jeanne D'Arc Francoise Michaud started out life on February 1, 1916, as Marie Choquette, the daughter of Dr. Omer Choquette of Ste. Agathe in Quebec. As a child, she was educated by the sisters at St. Jerome's Convent near Montreal. Marie left a strong impression on the nuns, who would later say she was one of their more talented pupils. Her skills as a pianist lead her to participate in radio programs around the area.

Marie was married to Laurent Michaud, when both of them were rather young, and soon had a child. After marriage, they settled for a time in the northern mining district of Abitibi, Quebec, before moving to the United States. Marie earned a bachelor's degree from a university in Montreal and was regarded as a competent linguist. Reports would later say Laurent returned to Abitibi.

In 1948, Marie was living in Madison, Wisconsin, with her husband, Laurent, who was in graduate school pursuing a degree in agriculture. They had their son living with them at 521 North Henry Street, a location then known as the Stone Lodge. Records suggest they only stayed one year. The couple would soon be divorced, with Laurent becoming a veterinarian and their son sent away to a private school "in the East."

The stylish sandstone Stone Lodge was built in 1851 by Judge Levi Baker Vilas. He was the fourth mayor of Madison and served three nonconsecutive years in the Wisconsin State Assembly, representing Dane County (greater Madison). While mayor, Vilas was determined to rid the city of dogs that ran at large, destroyed trees and made sidewalks unfit for use. He directed the police to shoot unleashed dogs on sight. The council ordered police officers who did not kill their quota of dogs to be fined. During the American Civil War, Vilas was a draft commissioner. He was one of the regents of the University of Wisconsin System and the Wisconsin Historical Society. His son was William Freeman Vilas, who served as United States postmaster general and in the United States Senate. (The Vilas family was prominent in Madison, and their name can be found on many public buildings, streets and more.) Following Vilas's passing, the home became a fraternity house for some years before switching over to general housing for students.

On the darker side was the story of Harold Kotvis and Adele Burnton Kotvis, who lived in the house in September 1934. They first met around 1931 while both were students at Ripon College. Then, in January 1934, they were married in a whirlwind by the justice of the peace in Waukegan and stayed two nights at the Hotel Wisconsin in Milwaukee for their honeymoon. Harold was the son of the postmaster at Hillsboro in southwest Wisconsin and a lieutenant in the army reserves, well respected and admired. Adele was the daughter of a fuel company president in Fond du Lac. But by September, Harold, unable to find employment other than as a poorly reimbursed teaching assistant, was being threatened with divorce by his wife. Frantic and panicked, he shot her dead and then shot himself—except that the shots were not as effective as he likely expected.

Adele was resting on a cot when the bullet entered the left side of her face, just below the eye. It exited the right side of her face, shattering her cheekbone, and was embedded in the mattress. Despite this, she held on for several hours before passing at Madison General Hospital. Harold turned the gun on himself and shot himself in

Top: Jeanne Michaud poses for the camera with a book. *Associated Press Wire photo*.

Bottom: Adele Kotvis, the innocent victim of a disturbed and dejected husband. *From the* Wisconsin State Journal.

the head, the bullet passing through his brain, coming out of his skull and lodging in the ceiling. These were the only two shots fired, with five left in the gun. Despite the profuse bleeding, Harold was still alive when he was rushed to the hospital, with fellow student Harry Sheer (sports editor of the school paper) on hand to provide a transfusion.

A note in Harold's pocket read,

> *This .45 automatic pistol is the property of Ray E. Searle of Ripon. I obtained it from him under the false pretense that I wished to do some target practice. Please see that this gun is returned to him or that he is reimbursed for it from my estate. The ammunition is some that I picked up while attending the ROTC camp at Ft. Sheridan in 1929. It is our wish that we be buried together in order that we may achieve eternally that which was denied us in life.*

His "last request" to be buried beside Adele was not honored by her family. She is in Fond du Lac, while he lies in Hillsboro. Until finding the marriage certificate in their room, her parents did not even realize she was married, and Adele's roommate Ada R. Dettwiler confided to them that it was something of a shotgun wedding: Harold had threatened to kill himself if she did not go through with it. Dettwiler was "not surprised" that Harold ended up killing himself but never thought he would kill Adele. Both funerals were abundantly attended, with over one hundred people in Harold's cortege and two pastors on hand.

Did the Michaud couple know of this past tragedy? Did the specter of grief haunt the halls of this stately manor? We do not know, and their time there was apparently uneventful. If we can speculate anything at all, it is that their time in Madison may not have been a happy one, as the marriage did not last long.

According to later news reports, Laurent and Marie received a divorce in Reno in 1949. With Reno offering the fastest divorces in the country, they no doubt went there for this reason exclusively, though Marie stayed on. After this, she moved into the Stardust guest ranch on Dickerson Road, operated by Russell R. and Linnie Smith. Michaud is shown living there on the 1950 census, along with another lodger, sixty-one-year-old widower Roy L. Park. Michaud also made the acquaintance of an older man named Benton Henry Robinson. According to the Smiths, she was "well put together" and "men found her attractive....Plenty of them were always waiting around to take her out."

Robinson was born in northeast Colorado and lived for many years in the Oakland area. In 1920, he was a proprietor of a hotel there. Robinson was married to Florence Sharpe, and they had two children, Betty and Eugene. Following the birth of their second child, the couple divorced, and Florence maintained custody of the children. She suffered from increasingly intense feelings of melancholia before finally taking her own life in 1929. After swallowing poison, she wrote three notes, which were found the next morning on her bedside:

> *To Whom It May concern: I, Florence S. Robinson, am taking a dose of poison, hoping to die as I suffer so much from melancholia. I have tried to fight it off, but it is no use. No one is to blame for my act. I have no ill feelings toward anyone. My friends and my family have all been wonderful to me. In case I don't die right away, call Dr. Clarence DePuy at 230 Grand Avenue. I'd rather have him attend me than a stranger. I want to be cremated and my ashes thrown in my sister's garden. F. Robinson*

The second letter reads,

> *It is my dying wish that Marie Bishop be made the guardian of my two children, Betty Jane and Eugene Channing, without bond. I leave all I have to her as she sees fit. —Florence S. Robinson, June 11, 1929*

Mrs. Bishop was Florence's sister, and Mrs. Robinson's children lived with her. A large envelope containing Mrs. Robinson's jewelry, money and other personal effects was found addressed to Mrs. Bishop.

The last note reads, "It is exactly 3:23. I hope I took enough. No pain, but my heart is pumping. Florie."

What caused Benton Robinson to be estranged from his ex-wife and children is unknown, but in 1925, he was already remarried, to LaVerne Webster. This marriage would be short-lived as well; LaVerne passed away in 1934 at only thirty-two years old. After this, Benton floated from boardinghouse to boardinghouse, working as an auto mechanic or machinist wherever he could find employment. Eventually, he made his way to Reno and met Michaud, whom he was instantly drawn to.

Robinson was staying at the Washoe Medical Center but had no friends or family. Russell Smith was also there, which led to Michaud making frequent visits. Somehow, she stumbled upon Robinson and began to visit him as well. Eventually, she was spending more time in Robinson's room than with Smith.

Michaud's new friend moved to the Stardust ranch at her suggestion. At first, he was a paying guest like anyone else. He was introduced to the Smiths as "Mr. Clark," and they accepted this. Over the next several months, according to Mrs. Smith, Robinson came to "worship" Michaud. She said their relationship was "like that between a loyal servant and a kind employer." Michaud "seemed to appreciate the attention, but didn't pay much attention to him." The Smiths became quite fond of them both.

Although stories vary, it appears that Michaud and Redfield met in April 1951 and immediately hit it off. Redfield would make bets for her at the Riverside casino that he considered "investments." According to Michaud, things soon turned romantic. While I tend to think this is correct, Redfield would not explicitly acknowledge such a connection. This would be the crux of a courtroom debate, as we will see later.

As Michaud told it, she decided to either get "revenge" on Redfield or try to cure him of his money addiction. Her motives are murky at best, but by the fall of 1951, she had set her sights on burglarizing the Redfield home and knew how it had to be done (more on this later). She reached out to Robert Gentle of Huntsville, Alabama, whom she had reason to believe would know people in the local underworld. Her "loyal servant" Robinson initially served as a middleman so no one could identify Michaud if things fell through.

Gentle suggested Anthony Gazzigli as someone who would be able to help. In retrospect, it is not clear how Gazzigli was chosen, and we have to wonder if Gentle meant someone else. Gazzigli had been a Reno resident since 1939 and had worked as a janitor at the Cal-Neva for the last two years but was no burglar. Regardless, Robinson called Gazzigli and told him to come out to the alley in five minutes. Gazzigli agreed, and Robinson approached him with a telegram from Gentle as a letter of introduction. Gazzigli hesitantly agreed to assemble a burglary team after Robinson (who never introduced himself) said the cash involved could be as much as $50,000. Anthony was married with three children and previously lived in Rochester, New York. His only prior arrests were in Rochester for truancy and "rolling a drunk." He was not, by any stretch, a man "connected" to the criminal element.

Though Gazzigli kept delaying, Robinson called him repeatedly until, finally, Robinson handed him a floor plan of the Reno home sketched by Michaud and pushed Gazzigli to get moving. The first incarnation of the heist crew was led by Claude Bernard Micheletti, whom Gazzigli knew only

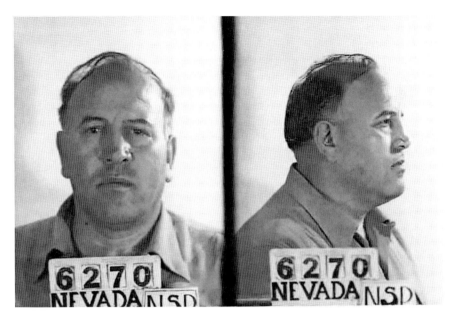

Louis Gazzigli, known to friends as "Firpo," after his burglary conviction. *Nevada State Prison.*

as "Dago Jack" from San Francisco. The less Gazzigli knew, the better he felt about it. Using the floor plan, Micheletti cased the mansion with Albert Bacon Bustamonte and Ralph M. Roberts. While prowling one night, they were "flushed out" by Nell Redfield, and they put the plan on hold. Gazzigli told Micheletti, "Just forget about the job, it is all off."

During all this, Michaud continued to see Redfield and travel between Reno and Hollywood as if nothing was amiss. On December 27, 1951, Michaud returned to Reno from Los Angeles. She had been trying to find a job as a television performer or, perhaps, find someone to purchase and record her songs. For the two months following her return, according to the family she stayed with, she never had a phone call and almost never left her room. The only person they believed she had any contact with besides Robinson was her son.

Were her housemates covering for her, or did they just not pay that much attention? Perhaps Michaud was particularly clever in her movements. Whatever the case, it soon became clear she was not the homebody they suggested she was. She was meeting with her proxies and keeping the plan in motion.

Robinson called Gazzigli out of the blue one day, telling him the house was "ripe again." Anthony Gazzigli, mansion diagram in hand, bumped into his brother Louis one afternoon when Louis was in the company of "Johnny" Triliegi. They were just exiting Joseph Hornstein's Nevada Turf Club. Triliegi's Reno visit was not merely to visit his friends, including Joseph George Scrivano—he was in town because Angeline Koremenos Wilcott was delivering his illegitimate baby. Anthony knew Triliegi's reputation and recognized instantly he was the man to lead the second incarnation of the burglary team. Just who was John Triliegi?

Chapter 4
THE SOAP SALESMAN

Giovanni Battista "John" Triliegi was born on May 20, 1914, in Omaha, Nebraska, to Bruno Triliegi and Concetta Trovato. What brought the Triliegis to Nebraska is not known, as most of their extended family lived in Queens, but while he was still young, John and family moved to Milwaukee. He would maintain contact with Omaha cousins throughout his life, but Milwaukee was home.

His life of crime started young. Triliegi, sixteen, was arrested for attempted auto larceny on April 17, 1931, and sent to the detention home, a correction center for boys. He was warned, and the matter was closed. On April 25, Triliegi was arrested again for aiding and advising the commission of a felony (a burglary). This time, on May 1, he was sent to the St. Charles Boys Home in Milwaukee for one year but did not serve the full time.

Triliegi was arrested for violations of the Prohibition Act on April 4, 1932. He was turned over to federal authorities the next day and released. Triliegi, now nineteen, was arrested on January 14, 1934, as an inmate of a gambling house and was fined five dollars. Gambling would be a constant in his life for over a decade, with the occasional pickup for vagrancy, a vague charge used by police to pick up men loitering near businesses, with no shopping agenda or work prospects.

At age twenty-five, he was arrested for "carnal knowledge and abuse" (statutory rape) on October 24, 1939. Triliegi pleaded guilty and was sentenced by Judge John Gregory to five years' probation. He had recently been married to Stefania Balestrieri, who somehow tolerated this behavior.

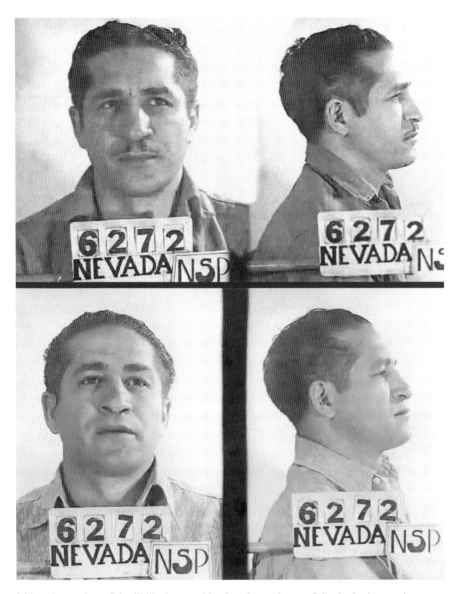

Milwaukee mobster John Triliegi, a gambler, burglar and more. Why he had two prison booking photos is unknown. *Nevada State Prison*.

Between 1943 and 1947, he was picked up at least five times for being in a gambling house, with one of those incidents ending in a $250 fine when he was named as the host.

The string of gambling arrests came from his association with the Ogden Social Club, a "floating" gambling operation that moved from house to house throughout the 1940s. While the club was often raided, moving locations kept the fines low—the "keeper" of the gambling operation was always different. Mafia up-and-comer Frank Balistrieri was rumored to be the club's "bank," but he was never charged.

Putting gambling behind him, or at least learning to avoid arrest, Triliegi took up work as a traveling soap salesman. Triliegi was picked up in Appleton, Wisconsin, on June 11, 1947, for peddling an inferior grade of soap and was ordered out of town by the police chief. Triliegi was arrested on a charge of disorderly conduct on June 18, 1950. He was carrying a sawed-off shotgun in his car. The charge was dismissed a month later.

Stepping back a bit, John Triliegi and his brother-in-law John Balestrieri had purchased the Riviera (401 North Plankinton) in November 1949. The place was originally opened around 1947 as the Anchor Inn, which catered to sailors. Whether or not it explicitly catered to the growing underground gay community, the homosexual subculture of navy life was already well-established. Carrying over to the new owners, the place had a reputation as a bar for gay men and hustlers (male sex workers). An ad in the December 21, 1949 *Milwaukee Journal Sentinel* called it "a new and different place for your wining and dining pleasure." The ad mentions "Chef 'Eli' and Waiter 'Leonard'" and states, "A famous chef and a noted bartender join their talents"; author Michail Takach suggests those may have been names familiar to gay men of the time.

While this may be the most interesting part of Triliegi's story up to this point, it was short-lived, and he managed to keep the operation completely under the radar. Tony Machi, around September 1951, took over the Riviera, offering thirty-five-cent martinis as the house specialty.

In late January 1952, John Triliegi was in Reno, where he hooked up with Louis "Firpo" Gazzigli, and this is when the plan was hatched. Triliegi brought into the loop safecracker Andrew Young. Readers should continue to the next chapter to return to the heist or read on for the rest of the Riviera story.

Mary Wathen operated Mary's, one of the city's first "gay for pay" bars, at 400 North Plankinton (across from the Riviera), from 1959 to 1960. Police chief Johnson advised against licensing as Mary's had attracted "undesirable elements." Wathen, according to one story, had tried to take over the Sunflower Inn from "Dirty Helen" Cromwell and opened Mary's as a backup plan. Another, more reliable version of the story says Mary was a front for her boyfriend, crooked finance man (read: loan shark) Harry Kaminsky, and she was appalled by the homosexual community—so much so that after a year she dumped Harry and moved west of the Mississippi. Harry then changed the name Mary's to the Black Nite—a club that is finally gaining recognition in Milwaukee (a Google search will lead you to some great research by Takach). You can read more about Cromwell in her autobiography, *Dirty Helen*.

A 1961 article from the *Milwaukee Journal Sentinel* illustrates harassment toward gay bar operators and patrons at the time. Judge Christ Seraphim fined Andrew Machi fifty dollars for permitting dancing at the Riviera. The defense's contention that the city ordinance banning public dancing was not violated because the three sets of dancers were men was rejected by the judge, who said, "This place caters to that kind of clientele." Peter Machi was also fined, but the charges against him were dismissed. Charges remained open against bartender Gerald Holtz, to be activated if anything happened again.

"On Sunday afternoons, the place was loaded with cops," said one contributor to Takach's book *LGBT Milwaukee*. "Sometimes, they'd bring their women, but rarely did they bring their wives." Patrons remember policemen visiting the Riviera's basement, which allegedly housed an illegal booking joint, and stuffing envelopes into their coat pockets on the way out.

Part owner Thomas Machi was robbed at 7:30 p.m. on March 13, 1961, by three unknown men, but he did not alert the police. His brother Tony reported the crime, and Thomas confirmed it but would not file a complaint. The three men knocked Thomas down while he was entering his garage, asked him his name, told him to keep quiet and then brought him back into the house. Inside, the men rummaged through Thomas's pockets and tied him to a chair. They searched the house and left with between $2,500 and $3,000, as well as a ring and gold cufflinks. Thomas said he did not want publicity but offered the police a whiskey bottle the men had drunk from to be checked for fingerprints.

On April 25, an informant told the FBI he suspected a Milwaukee person ordered the robbery but it was to have been carried out by Chicago men. The FBI noted the Riviera was a "hangout for sexual perverts."

Tony Machi was interviewed by Special Agent Richard Thompson at his home on August 31, 1962, around noon. Thompson specifically timed the visit to coincide with peak horse-betting time and noted that no phone calls came in while they were there. Tony said his brother Peter was the licensee on the Riviera, but all the Machi brothers had a stake in it and worked there. The tavern opened daily at 5:00 p.m. Machi told Thompson he'd lived his whole life in Milwaukee and had never been shaken down by anyone or by any syndicate. Regarding the robbery of his brother, he said he did not know who was responsible but did not believe it was any syndicate.

On September 17, 1962, a detective from the Milwaukee Police Department Special Squad spoke with the FBI concerning the Machi brothers. He said he had some "mental reservations" about one of the bartenders at the Riviera because this bartender hung out with the sons of known Mafia members Joseph Gurera, Peter Balistrieri and Frank Balistrieri. The detective said that years ago, Isadore Tocco and the Machis were bookies above the Produce Building on Broadway but no longer worked together. The detective said the Machis denied they paid off Joseph Gurera and the syndicate, but he was confident that they did.

According to a report the police turned over to the FBI on November 19, businesses suspected of paying "insurance" to the mob were the Holiday House, Sardino's, the Riviera and Fazio's. The Scaffidi Brothers Bakery on East Brady Street was also said to have recently been shot up by some men, and the bakery did not report the incident to police but instead decided to go out of business.

Thomas Machi was interviewed by Special Agent Thompson on December 3 at his residence to see if he had been the victim of a shakedown by Joseph Gurera. Machi acknowledged he knew Gurera, saying they had met at a tavern a while back and had seen each other occasionally at Gallagher's, a club operated by mob boss Frank Balistrieri. Machi said they played golf together once, but he denied knowing what Gurera did for a living and said he had not threatened Machi in any way. Machi denied making payoffs to any syndicate and said if he were to be approached, he would inform the authorities. He told the FBI that when he was robbed, $1,000 was taken from his pockets and another $2,500 from his home. His parents were home at the time, and they were tied up, too. Machi suspected the robbery was ordered by a local man and was committed by three men from out of town, but he claimed not to know who.

On March 15, 1964, the Riviera burned down. The FBI noted that although the cause appeared to be arson, the Machis were probably not behind it, as the tavern was underinsured and a moneymaking "fag joint." The catastrophic five-alarm fire consumed the Riviera and devastated the block. "I was on vacation in California," said a contributor to *LGBT Milwaukee*, "when someone called me to say, 'Your house is on fire—come home!'" At 6:00 p.m., someone ran into the bar and yelled, "Fire!" Bartender Richard Dupont Isensee remained open until policemen ordered him to evacuate. "When we left, the ceiling was on fire," said Isensee. "But you just don't leave a dirty bar." The ruins smoldered for a week. Rumor has it that a lovers' spat ended with one of the men setting fire to the building, but the truth will likely never be known.

The FBI interviewed Tony Machi on April 28 at his residence. He said the Riviera had been a financial success and that the loss of this tavern was a setback because it was not insured; without insurance, Machi had to pay $19,000 out of pocket. This would be the end for the Riviera.

Now, back to our regularly scheduled programming.

Chapter 5
THE INNOCENT KILLER?

A ndrew Robert Young (or sometimes *Andreis* Robert Young) was not your stereotypical criminal. He did not grow up in poverty, lacking opportunities, or come from a broken home or anything else you would point to as the "Aha!" cause for delinquency. He seemingly had every chance to become a respected member of the community but went another direction. Rebellion? An innate desire for thrills? The reader is left to ponder. Years later, a psychologist said his delinquency stemmed from being "mentally depraved" with a "morbid impulsiveness."

Andrew was born in Springfield, Illinois, on November 14, 1906, the second of four sons. His father, Edward, was a laborer in a brickyard at the time of his birth but by 1920 had taken up employment with the city as a firefighter. Edward would maintain this position throughout his adult life and was well liked and respected in Illinois's capital city.

Around 1922, at fifteen years old, Andrew Young dropped out of high school. At the same time, he had a tonsillectomy. From then on, he maintained no steady employment, picking up odd jobs here and there. Young's longest stint was as a meter assembler, a job he held for two years with incredibly poor performance and attendance. He often indulged in liquor during Prohibition and was sexually promiscuous. On at least one occasion, in 1925, he had to be treated for gonorrhea. Choosing "unsavory companions" over law-abiding ones opened his eyes to the world of crime.

In the late evening of March 19, 1927, all was well in Sheboygan, Wisconsin—very much a small town, an hour north of Milwaukee, where everything was usually quiet and residents had no fear. Then a strange incident was followed by a tragic one.

First, at around 11:30 p.m., Arno Carl Kremin was on his way home when he noticed a young man with a gray cap and dark overcoat looking into the windows at 1718 South Tenth Street. Kremin happened to live in an upstairs apartment, so he crept around to a back door and alerted the ground-floor resident, Sidney Pelkofer, of what was going on. Together they tried to ambush the peeper but were too late to catch him in the act. The police were called, and they arrived in the "special police car." The neighborhood was searched, as far away as Otto Kohls' tavern, but the young man could not be found. Police picked up one suspicious character, but Kremin denied he was the peeper and nothing more could be done.

Tragedy struck just before midnight at Otto Kohls's tavern at 1223 Broadway, known as the Cuckoo's Nest. Two bandits rounded up the people present and robbed them, forcing them to turn their pockets out. The victims included Walter Kohls, Otto Kohls, Fred Burrow and Frank Stahl. Olaf Jonassen was the unlucky one: lunging at one of the gunman when he saw an opening, he was riddled with bullets before the two crooks fled. Altogether they managed to collect $200, two watches and two knives.

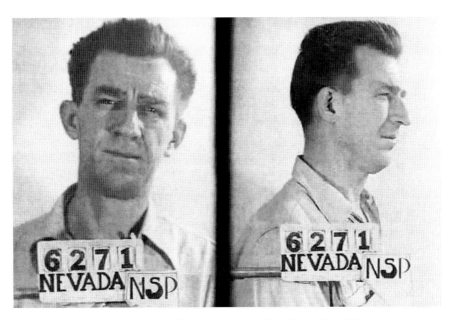

Andrew Robert Young, convicted killer and armed robber. *Nevada State Prison.*

The following afternoon, farmer William E. Meggers alerted police of a Nash coupe that was stuck in the mud near his property. The location was described as in the town of Wilson, south of Sheboygan, three quarters of a mile east of Rudolph Turk's roadhouse on Highway 17. Meggers had not heard about the Sheboygan murder and, because of this, had not called the police sooner. Abandoned cars in the mud were fairly common in the area, so this one did not seem suspicious. Deputies Ernst Zehms and Connie Juckem arrived and found bloodstains in the car and on the running board, leading them to conclude this must be the getaway vehicle. Their belief was confirmed when the license plate was traced back to Dr. Joseph W. Steckbauer, who reported his car stolen in Manitowoc a few hours before the tavern shooting.

A bloody Chicago newspaper from March 17 was found inside, wrapped around various items, including two empty pocketbooks, two pocketknives, a package of toothpaste, a package of shaving cream, a small can of face powder, a bottle of toilet water, a safety razor, a toothbrush and four unused red handkerchiefs. Several empty .32-caliber shells were scattered around. A closer examination of the bloodstains in the car led investigators to believe they were transferred there from bloody clothes. In other words, it was more likely Jonassen's blood than that of the killers. Luckily for Dr. Steckbauer, the car was completely unharmed; once removed from the mud, the engine operated as normal. When Steckbauer examined the vehicle, he found that even the items he had left in there, doctors' tools and a flashlight, were untouched.

Sheriff Paul Schmidt had his men search the area for signs that the bandits had broken into any nearby cottages. As they were on foot and possibly injured, the sheriff expected they could not travel far. His men set up a base at the Jerving farm east of the Black River parallel to Lake Michigan and scoured the area for broken locks and windows or fresh footprints in the mud. No clues were discovered.

The investigation was still going strong at the end of March, with clues leading officers far and wide. Locally, Manitowoc, Fort Atkinson, Outagamie County and St. Nazianz were scoured and farther away, Milwaukee, Chicago and Elgin, Illinois. Along the way, police found some Michigan bank robbers and broke up a Manitowoc gang but could not locate Jonassen's killers. Their attention was drawn to a man staying in a Chicago hospital, but eyewitnesses said the patient was innocent.

Not much later, on April 18, 1927, our subject Andrew Young and his companion Frank Alveust Allgood robbed a shoe store in Bloomington,

Illinois. Caught shortly after, they were arrested and put on trial. A gun in their possession was tested and matched up with one that fired the bullets into Jonassen, implicating one or both men in his murder. Chief Wagner, Walter Kohls, Otto Kohls, Fred Burrow and Frank Stahl all traveled to Illinois and made a positive identification of the two men. A knife found in their possession was also identified as one belonging to Burrow.

Allgood appears to have had a challenging childhood based on the paper trail he left behind. He was born November 1901 in Springfield, Illinois, and his father passed away less than a year later. Allgood's mother soon remarried, but for reasons unknown, she either could not or would not raise Frank. The 1910 census shows him, his brother John and their sister Annie being raised by nuns at an orphanage in Alton, Illinois. The experience was perhaps a positive one for Annie, who pursued a nursing career. John became a coal miner and died at only twenty-one years old. Frank would spend his life in a series of institutions, which brings us back to our narrative.

While it would seem to make more sense to try the men for the more serious crime of murder first, that was not how their legal journey played out. The robbery trial came first, and after the jury returned a guilty verdict in May, Judge Edward Barry of McLean County sentenced both men to "ten years to life" in Joliet state prison. Murder warrants were served on the prisoners, but they would not take effect until they were released from Joliet—potentially never. The Jonassen family would not see justice any time soon.

The way the newspapers tell the story, another victim of the Jonassen murder was Olaf's father, Ole Jonassen, seventy-one. Ole "brooded over his son's death, was unable to take proper nourishment, and his physical condition became weakened." He had been a brave man in his youth, visiting all corners of the world as a Norwegian sailor in the days before modern conveniences, but this shock was too much. Gangrene poisoning set in, and doctors had to amputate his leg in May 1928. This was not enough, and two weeks later, Ole died of his malady in a Sheboygan hospital.

The next victim was Otto Kohls, forty, owner of the "soft drink parlor" where Jonassen was killed. Kohls was on vacation at Round Lake with his friends Frank Stahl (another witness) and William Spuds when a sudden illness overtook him. A local doctor suggested getting him back to Sheboygan, and on arrival at the hospital around 12:30 a.m. on August 26, 1929, Kohls was pronounced dead. Friends said he had "been in a nervous condition" ever since the robbery, and this no doubt contributed to his decline in health. Kohls had fought in World War I as part of the 127th Infantry, Fourth

Division, and was honored by countless people at his funeral, including by his parents, who survived him.

On October 26, 1939, after serving twelve years in Joliet prison for the Bloomington robbery, Young was freed, only to be brought to Sheboygan to face trial for the Jonassen killing. Sheriff Ernst Zehms (a deputy ten years prior), Undersheriff Walter Knopp and Detective William Rothe drove from Sheboygan to Joliet and back to transport Young. The time between the crime and the trial could only have helped him: memories fade, and one witness (Kohls) had passed away. Frank Allgood remained in prison for now.

Young's defense attorney, Harvard-educated Jacob A. Fessler, traveled to the state prison at Joliet on December 1, 1939, in order to take a deposition from Allgood. It would later be revealed that Allgood himself requested such an interview. Present also, representing the State of Wisconsin, was Sheboygan assistant district attorney Richard Barrett.

On December 20, 1939, Judge Henry Arthur Detling denied a defense motion seeking the dismissal of the case against Young. Defense attorney Jacob Fessler read the deposition taken from Frank Allgood that it was another man named "Short Arm" Louis George Schomber, not Young, who had been the shooter in the Jonassen murder. Allgood went into detail about where he (Allgood) acquired different guns and who had possession of them, explaining that he had the murder weapon prior to the Bloomington holdup. Young had not joined him until a week prior to that, when they met by happenstance and stole a car. Fessler maintained that Young was at his home in Springfield, Illinois, at the time of the Jonassen murder. Detling denied the dismissal, countering that eyewitness Fred Burrow of Sheboygan put Young at the scene of the crime. Schomber had passed away and could not confirm Allgood's claim.

Following the guilty verdict, Young made a motion for a new trial, which Detling denied. Young was sentenced to life in prison on December 20. Detling said the law made the punishment for first-degree murder a mandatory life sentence, so he had no power to give out any other option. When asked if he had anything to say, Young—described as "tall" and "sandy-haired"—could only mumble, "No, sir." Detling informed him, "The jury finds that you were here in Sheboygan on the night of the murder of Olaf Jonassen, and I believe it, too. You have had a fair trial and a good defense, but the truth prevailed." According to the local newspaper, this was the first life sentence ever given out in Sheboygan County's long history.

Perhaps due to his long run in the Illinois prison, Young adjusted well to life in Waupun. An April 26, 1940 report said he was of average intelligence and attended the in-prison school. He was a reader and had a mental age of 15.25 years, with no signs of psychosis. Perusing the prison library seemed to take up much of his time, as he had no work assignments in his first several months and did not attend any church services. Young left a positive impression on those around him: they described him as "affable" despite his rather shallow, superficial personality. He was "frank" with the authorities, admitting to every crime on his record, though steadfastly denying any connection to the Jonassen murder. He admitted his actions in life were in "direct contrast" to the environment in which he was raised. In fact, he pointed to this as evidence of his innocence. His father, highly respected in Springfield, had provided him an alibi for the Jonassen murder. It's one thing for a career criminal to deny wrongdoing, but his father was putting his very reputation on the line.

A physical examination by Dr. Austin Joseph Hebenstreit revealed nothing overly remarkable about Young. He had a deviated septum to the right (common in people who have played contact sports or been involved in any rough activity) and chronic moderate psoriasis but was otherwise in good health. He had prominent scapuli (collarbones), a tendency toward "pigeon breast" (pectus carinatum, a protrusion of the chest over the sternum described as birdlike) and flat feet. His teeth were moderately "carious" (decayed), with several missing. Oddly, a metallic *click* could occasionally be heard "over apex of mitral area" (left of the heart), with no explanation. Young had several tattoos, but these were not described by Dr. Hebenstreit.

On July 15, 1941, Frank Allgood, now thirty-nine, completed his fourteen-year term for armed robbery at the Illinois State Prison and was immediately taken into custody by police chief Walter Wagner and brought to Sheboygan. Allgood waived his right to a preliminary hearing before Judge Edward Harold Puhr and was held without bail. Before trial, Allgood pleaded guilty to murder and, on August 11, was sentenced to twenty-five years in prison by Judge Detling. Allgood and Young were once more reunited, with Young as inmate no. 25321 and Allgood no. 26505. By this time, Young had established himself as trustworthy, and some reports say he even worked as the warden's chauffeur on occasion.

The warden, incidentally, made no public claims to believing whether Young was guilty of murder or not. However, in a November 1942 report, he expressed concern that regardless of the guilt question, he felt that there might be some inequity at play. The report noted that Frank Allgood, who was positively involved in the murder, was sentenced to twenty-five years on a second-degree plea. Meanwhile, Young was sentenced to life on a first-degree charge, though some doubt about his involvement persisted. Was it fair that Allgood received a lighter sentence? In the eyes of the court, Young likely was given a longer sentence because he refused to "accept responsibility" for his actions, but what if he had no responsibility to accept?

Young applied for pardon in 1943 but was unsuccessful. On September 30, he received a brief note from pardon secretary Margaret E. Pollock saying only, "This is to advise you that Governor Goodland today denied your petition for executive clemency."

Undaunted, Young wrote to Governor Walter Samuel Goodland again in September 1944 and swore his innocence before notary public Edwin H. Krause. He acknowledged, "I have now served over seventeen years in prison, and under my present sentence must serve a total of twenty-four years before being eligible for parole." Despite this, Young laid out how Allgood received a lighter sentence than him and stressed that affidavits had named the "real killer" as "Louis Schomberg" [sic]. Young explained, "Upon investigation by my attorney, Jacob Fessler, it was found that Schomberg had died on May 23, 1939, just a few months before my trial. As a result, during my trial, it appeared as if I was trying to blame a crime on a dead man. Which I assure you was not the case."

Young continued, explaining that Allgood never talked about Sheboygan while the pair were in Joliet prison. Then, unexpectedly, Allgood wrote to Fessler shortly before trial. This was the first time Young ever heard the name of the real killer. If Young is to be believed, Allgood was refusing to "rat" on his buddy Schomber, but this became moot once he was dead. Young wrote,

At the time of my arrest in Illinois, I was twenty years old. I had no previous convictions. Due to this charge in Wisconsin, I was obliged to serve six years and two months more than the usual time for a first offender in similar cases. I am now thirty-eight years of age. Although I am not guilty of this charge, I believe that after all that has happened it is practically impossible for me to prove my innocence.

Throwing himself on the mercy of the governor, he concluded,

It is my firm belief that the sentence meted out to me, in view of the circumstances, was excessive and severe. So I ask and hope that you will commute my sentence to twenty-five years or any other clemency that your Excellency may deem fitting and proper.

Interestingly, despite maintaining his innocence, Young approached the governor with humility—asking only a reduction in time rather than the release from prison he felt would be the correct decision.

The results of Young's final examination on September 14, 1945, again presented him in a generally positive light. Dr. Peter Bell said he was

> *rather self-effacing, definitely stable, well-mannered, mildly self-conscious and generally imbued with a makeup which indicates his earlier exposure to an environment better in type than average. He is possessed of good mental endowment. His faculties are keen, and he displays reasoning and judgment of good nature.*

Young was said to have no "innate viciousness" and never antagonized the prison's law enforcement but instead cooperated however possible, despite his insistence he was wrongly imprisoned. Bell was sympathetic to Young and noted that because he was in an Illinois prison more than a decade before being tried in Sheboygan, records that would have exonerated him (such as time cards showing him punched in at work) were destroyed during the long wait. Bell took it upon himself to repeatedly question Frank Allgood, and the story he received was always the same: Young was innocent, and the killer was Louis Schomber. Though Bell never said as much, the report suggests he believed Young was innocent or at least had strong doubts about his guilt.

Governor Goodland gave Young an "absolute" pardon on January 5, 1946, setting him free from a life sentence after only six years. Immediately after his pardon, Young moved to Springfield, Illinois. According to Francis Lamb, the governor's pardon counsel, a motivating factor was an affidavit signed by Frank Allgood saying that Young was not at the murder scene but rather the man was Louis Schomber. The same claim that Judge Detling found unpersuasive at trial was enough to get Young out.

On January 21, 1946, Judge Detling filed a formal objection to Governor Goodland's statement that "an innocent man had been convicted" in the Jonassen slaying. Speaking to the press, Detling said he had no objection to a pardon if Young had been rehabilitated or exhibited good conduct; however, "I do not want the case to go down in history as one in which an innocent man has been convicted. I am satisfied that the jury's verdict was sound and that Young was convicted justly." Detling brought up the claim that Young had been given some sort of "truth serum" and maintained his innocence while under its influence, but Detling insisted the use of truth serum "is something experimental, to say the most for it, and less useful or reliable after a lapse of years. It is an experiment or procedure not even recognized in the trial of cases."

Although an Illinois native, Young moved to Milwaukee after his release. He married Pauline Banczak, a young mother, and tried his hand at being a father to her children. Yet his lifelong impulse for crime and excitement betrayed him.

Chapter 6

BURGLARY

In January 1952, Triliegi and Louis Gazzigli drove to Milwaukee and spent some time there, at one point sending a letter to Tony Gazzigli in Reno letting them him know they had signed up a safecracker to the crew. This, of course, was Andrew Young. While in Milwaukee, Louis attended a trial "about some kind of car deal" that Triliegi had an interest in. (The records quoting Louis do not elaborate on what this meant, and readers are left to speculate.)

Triliegi, Gazzigli and Young drove to Reno in Triliegi's gray 1951 Cadillac and arrived on the morning of February 27, when Triliegi applied for a position as a card dealer. Frank Sorrenti came with them, serving as Triliegi's driver. The plan was to stay only a few days, but any income, for even a day or two, couldn't hurt. At 10:00 a.m., Triliegi and Sorrenti registered at the Carlton Hotel with desk clerk Charles L. Cornberger. They then went to the roof of the Cal-Neva to consult with Tony.

On February 29, despite the guest house operator's claim that Michaud had no callers and did not leave home, she was in downtown Reno at least for a little while. By sheer coincidence, she bumped into LaVere Redfield as he was leaving the post office on Virginia Street. He later explained, "I hadn't seen Mrs. Michaud in some time and I said, 'Well, this is a surprise.' I got the impression she was waiting for someone, so after I chatted with her for a minute or two, I went on." She apparently *was* waiting for someone, and as soon as Redfield left her view, she gave a signal to Tony Gazzigli. Redfield was out, and it was time to go.

During those ninety or so minutes between seeing Michaud and going home, LaVere was at Mert Wertheimer's Riverside, enjoying lunch with his wife, Nell. After the meal, LaVere played a quick round of roulette and Nell attended a fashion show in progress at the hotel.

At Redfield's house, Michaud's hired thieves broke in effortlessly through the rear kitchen door on the house's south side. They got around without making noise by feeding Redfield's dog Mac, a Kerry blue terrier, a ham hock that they found in the refrigerator and tying his leash to the closet door in Nell's bedroom. The thieves stole a four-hundred-pound green Mosler safe containing $1.5–2.5 million in currency, securities and gems from the northeast bedroom closet. A battered suitcase near the safe, containing another $1 million in securities, was overlooked.

Anthony Gazzigli, one of two brothers who found themselves part of the burglary ring. *From the Reno Evening Gazette.*

LaVere and Nell Redfield returned house at 2:00 p.m. and quickly realized that something was wrong. A broken mop and crowbar lay outside the back door. LaVere walked to 1461 Forest Street (a mere one hundred feet away), the home of Lester A. Grisham, who was outside repairing his fence, and asked if he saw anyone suspicious. Grisham said no, so Redfield returned and tried to open the door. He found that the lock was damaged and the door opened easily without a key. LaVere returned to the Grisham residence and had Edith Grisham call the police while he waited outside for them to arrive. He would later say he only called because he feared the burglars were still inside the house and were hurting his dog. Had he heard friendly barking, the whole matter would have gone unreported.

When asked about the incident, Redfield told reporters he had been "pretty stupid" to keep so much money in his house. He was still surprised that anyone was able to find the safe in "its inconspicuous position," which only he and his wife knew; the hiding place was in a front bedroom closet, buried beneath suitcases and clothing. "I am not feeling sorry for myself," he said. Insurance? "That's another foolish thing I didn't do. They can have the money as long as they didn't kill my little dog." Reporters asked Redfield what his dog's name was. "I can't tell you that," he replied. "He's ashamed of it."

Young was supposed to break into the safe on-site but failed, and he had to drag it out of the house into the trunk of Triliegi's Cadillac. Triliegi had joined him on the job but, because of a back injury, was likely not very helpful in moving the safe. The dragging action left red marks, likely rust, on the home's linoleum floors. Outside, footprints and tire tracks were left in the clay for detectives to trace.

Young and Triliegi met up with Tony Gazzigli, parked on Arlington Avenue nearby, who was surprised to see they had the entire safe with them. They drove in two vehicles to William Johnson's ranch on South Virginia, where Louis Gazzigli had been staying to hide out from one Nick Stassi, who had accused him of stealing whiskey. The safe was stashed in a spot under the house, and Young was left behind to stand watch while the other two, Triliegi and Tony Gazzigli, returned to town. Tony did not trust Young alone, but he feared Young would shoot Louis if Tony agitated him. While Triliegi and Tony Gazzigli were gone, Young burned his coat in the fireplace when he realized he had lost a button at the Redfield home. After dark, Triliegi and Tony Gazzigli returned and dragged the safe once more, this time to the barn, where they beat the safe until it broke open. In fact, Tony was dropped off by Michaud, but she drove away in Russell Smith's Hudson so no one would see her.

The safe's contents were carried into the kitchen and counted, with the total reaching $154,000. Bill Johnson arrived with an older man, Bill Wells. They jokingly knocked on the door pretending to be police, and Young pulled out a gun and pointed it at the door. Gazzigli, knowing the voices, motioned for Young to stop and called out that they had women in the house and Johnson should come back later.

Following the burglary, that same evening, Frank Sorrenti left Reno alone in Triliegi's Cadillac, driving first to Sacramento and then to Milwaukee. Triliegi left by train on March 1, a day before his hotel reservation expired.

Louis Gazzigli rented a delivery truck and told Johnson he was hauling rubbish to be dumped in an old mine shaft. The safe was loaded into the truck and taken away. By March 3, Louis had fled Reno and was staying with his girlfriend Louise Stacey in Sacramento.

Where was Andrew Young? We shall see.

Chapter 7

INVESTIGATION

T he only two clues left behind were a brown button and a miniature soap wrapper that came from the St. James Hotel in Davenport, Iowa. The police said burglars sometimes used soap to plant explosive charges, but in this instance that may not have been the case—the entire safe had been removed, with skid marks on the carpet where the thieves dragged the monstrous thing through the house. Perhaps the soap was used to decrease the friction, police speculated. Sisters Ruby and Marie Neely, maids at two neighboring properties, had seen a badly scratched dark green pickup truck at Redfield's home but could not further describe the vehicle and saw no one with it. Following this sighting, numerous other neighbors reported a green pickup in the area. Any owner of such a vehicle was now a suspect.

Chief Lorenz Greeson and Sheriff George Weaver Lothrop told the media that the best they could probably do at the moment was wait for something to happen. On March 1, the preliminary accounting was made public, with the safe said to include jewelry worth $50,000 to $100,000; more than $300,000 in cash, much of it in large denominations and a style of bill no longer in common use; and negotiable securities worth somewhere between $1 million and $2 million. Redfield, the police and the press focused on the upper range of all three estimates, a total of $2.4 million, which they declared would be the biggest burglary in American history.

Not reported to the press was that the safe also contained an Ortgies dark steel, fully loaded semiautomatic 7.65mm pistol with a wooden handle. Perhaps this information was withheld in the hopes that the police could later trace the gun, though Redfield had no record of any serial number.

The jewelry, heirlooms belonging to Redfield's friend Louise Hecker Root, was the only part of the loot that was insured. These jewels had first been insured in 1943 when they were used against a loan in Nome, Alaska, of all places. The pieces' primary purpose seemed to be to serve as collateral for other investments. Root had the jewels reappraised by Sam Ginsburg of Reno in June 1950 before signing the collection over to Redfield. Stetson and Beemer, the insurance company, provided police with a detailed list of thirty-two pieces of gold, platinum and diamond jewelry. The lot was insured for $54,257, or roughly $698,000 in today's dollars. (Police reports indicate that Root "stood much to gain" by the theft thanks to her insurance, but she was never seriously considered a suspect.)

At 10:30 a.m., Sergeant Bill Gregory spoke with Nell Redfield, focusing on prowlers she had seen recently near her house. She estimated the date to be December 1 and said that two men were crawling along the wall of her property around 6:00 p.m. while she was listening to Walter Winchell. Being home alone, she first considered calling a neighbor but then thought this might lead to someone being shot. Instead, she turned on her outside light, and this was enough to scare them off. She said the same two men returned the next night; they looked like they were thirty to thirty-five years old and were dressed in tan overcoats. Nell believed she had seen the same men outside two more times since then. Sometimes she received phone calls, but the caller usually hung up as soon as she said, "Hello?" Nell did say that one time a man responded, "Are you a good dame?" but he sounded more drunk than nefarious. Following the burglary, she found a crowbar outside, but no prying had been done to the door—she was sure they accessed the house with a passkey. From a display of photographs, she picked out Russell Foote Johnston, a Whittlesea Cab driver, as looking like one of the men.

Johnston was picked up and brought to the station. He worked part time at Whittlesea and part time as a station agent for United Airlines and had lived in Reno for the past six months with his wife and two children. Johnston said his landlord had a green pickup and he (Johnston) did drive it on occasion but had not done so in weeks. He further conceded he knew the Redfield home, although he had never been there, because he had briefly roomed with his coworker Scott Haynes at 1681 Arlington Avenue, about half a mile away. Although there were some interesting coincidences, Johnston's taxi fare schedule gave him a strong alibi. Unknown to him, Nell Redfield was watching the interrogation through a two-way mirror, and she also no longer felt he was a suspect.

The only other suspect LaVere and Nell Redfield would offer police was Norma Evonne Odenbach Gorman, a maid they had hired eight years ago but who had since moved to Alameda, California. Gorman, they said, was the only person who would have known about the existence of the safe. Further, she was known to have had an ex-con boyfriend, Robert Henninger, who was stationed at the Stead Air Force Base. Perhaps she told him and he waited for the right moment to strike?

Spencer Duane Redfield and David J. Schillinglaw, relatives of LaVere Redfield, were questioned because they had been present when the safe was installed fifteen years earlier and therefore knew of its existence. They were not considered suspects and were both in Los Angeles during the burglary. Spencer was another child of LaVere's brother Fred.

Police took a wrong turn on March 3, publicly naming five suspects in Butte, Montana, whom they believed to have committed the burglary. The group was linked to Reno because they were in regular contact with a prostitute named Sherry Rogers who hung out at the Mapes Hotel. The authorities named Geraldine Harris (described in the press as a "frightened, shapely blonde"), Floyd Dwight Dugger, Rodney Clinton Unger, Walter Earl Moore and Bendel Lee Moore. They were said to be driving two Cadillacs with Florida and Oklahoma license plates and heading for San Francisco. At the end of questioning, the group of "flashily-dressed men" and their female companion were ordered to leave the state. Their alibi was rock-solid: they had been in the Elko, Nevada jail during the burglary.

According to an anonymous tip, the safe was dumped in a lake fifty miles from Reno, near the Lahonton Dam in Fallon. This information originated from a phone call made by a man who declined to go on record, and the tip was wrong in every respect. Officer Clendenning of Reno and Sheriff Tower of Fernly scoured the area and found tire tracks in the sand and snow but no safe.

March 3 also brought Redfield's first public statement beyond his initial reaction. Concerning the burglary, he said, "It was a rotten trick." However, his concern was not so much about the money but the publicity that followed.

I am a marked man now. My privacy is gone. They did a far worse harm in that than in taking my money. Money can be replaced. There are many things in life that are more important than money. I have good health. I have a good wife and, with apologies to the (Irving Berlin) song—I have her love to keep me warm. Who can ask for anything more? I buy a bargain when I see one. If I can save a nickel on an item, I buy it in quantity, thus saving one or two dollars. If I hadn't done that all my life, I'd be just like so many other people today—just one step ahead of the bill collector. I can say that I don't owe a cent to anyone in the world, including Uncle Sam. If the internal revenue people will check their files, they'll find I have paid income taxes on far more money than was taken the other day.

On that last point, he may have protested too much.

Along with the publicity came attention from federal authorities. J. Edgar Hoover ordered agents to take a look at the case. At this point, no federal violation was known to have occurred, but if more than $5,000 crossed state lines, Hoover wanted his men to be there for an arrest. Chief Greeson was confident in his men and their abilities, saying, "We're checking and chasing leads. If we were getting close, we couldn't make it public anyway." Within a matter of days, FBI Special Agent D.K. Brown arrived from Salt Lake City, bringing with him roughly one dozen personnel, both agents and office staff, as well as some specialized equipment. With the local and federal authorities combined, it was believed as many as forty men were actively working on the case.

When the press spoke to Redfield, they seemed more interested in his roulette habits than the burglary. On March 5, he told them, "Gambling is bad. You can't beat the odds. It's all right for me to do it, because I can afford to lose." Exactly one month later he made similar remarks, saying, "I know I can't beat roulette. I never play for more than $30,000 at a time." Real estate broker Preston Quincy Hale confirmed that Redfield's nightly average seemed to be around $25,000. For those curious, $30,000 in 1952 is roughly the same as $349,000 today. He was dropping in one night what many people won't see in ten years.

The case made a major step forward on March 5, only days after the burglary—and much sooner than ever revealed publicly. While on patrol at 2:30 p.m., Officer James Franklin saw Albert Bacon Bustamante walking on East Commercial Row. Franklin called the man over and said they were going for a ride. As they drove around Reno, Franklin told Bustamante that he thought Bustamante was the sort of person who could probably identify the Redfield burglars. Bustamante agreed and said he would call Franklin at home after making the rounds of his usual hangouts. The police reports do not go into the prior relationship between Franklin and Bustamante, but it seems clear they had more than a passing familiarity with one another.

Around 9:30 p.m., Bustamante called Franklin at home. Franklin left in his personal car to pick up Bustamante, and they drove out to Wingfield Park.

With pencil and paper, Bustamante drew a fairly accurate diagram of the Redfield house layout and described the interior accurately. He explained to Franklin that months earlier, he met a man at the bar of the Golden Hotel who told him of an upcoming burglary, saying he expected to get a total of $40,000 or so from the job. The man was described as six feet tall, 185 pounds, with dark brown hair and wearing a topcoat, a hat and a diamond ring on his ring finger. He was perhaps in his mid-thirties. Bustamante said he did not know the man's name but would ask around and try to find it.

The next day, March 6, Bustamante called Franklin and arranged to meet him on the second floor of the post office at 2:00 p.m. Bustamante had either been holding back or had a very productive evening, because he now knew a great deal more. He said a man from Sacramento he knew only as "Three Finger Jack" or "Dago Jack" was originally in on the job, going so far as to case the house, and was upset that he was left out of the burglary. The layout of the house came from Tony Gazzigli, who was working with a woman who had been a "constant visitor" at the Redfield home. Bustamante further knew that Tony's brother "Firpo" was involved and that they had imported two men from Milwaukee to do the job. He suggested that if the police wiretapped Tony's phone, they would likely find where the other men were. Further, it was quite possible some of the stolen money was still in Tony's house. Clearly people were talking when they shouldn't be talking.

Redfield spoke to the press again on March 7, saying,

There is a likelihood I may quit my gambling....Everyone knows who I am now. I could come and go as I wished and not many people knew who I was. Now everyone will know my identity. They will follow me when I gamble. I don't want to be the goat leading the sheep. I know you can't always win at gambling. I gamble because it gives me relaxation and entertainment. I can afford to gamble and nobody goes hungry because I do. It hasn't gotten to be a disease with me, but I'm thinking about giving it up. I guess I'll have to find something else to do.

Although declining to offer a reward for the return of his property, Redfield said he would "pay liberally" for the return of the safe and its contents. This offer included the robbers. "I'm not one to expect something for nothing," he said.

Reno casino owners said Redfield was a "system gambler" and knew what he was doing with roulette. He had unlimited credit offered to him and, on the whole, had won more than he lost. It was not unusual for him to exchange a $100,000 check for one hundred $1,000 chips and come away with more. One club owner who declined to be identified said, "That Redfield is the smartest man who ever walked into my casino." One anonymous gambler joked, "Most of the money he lost (in the burglary) belongs to me—I feel as bad about it as he does!"

Albert Bustamante reached out to Officer Franklin again on March 7 and expressed a desire to speak directly to LaVere Redfield. Despite the unusual request, Franklin called Redfield, and he agreed to meet with Bustamante. They drove to the Redfield home, where Bustamante spoke with Redfield privately for over an hour. At the end of the visit, Bustamante waited in the car, and Franklin spoke to Redfield. The burglary victim declined to say what had been discussed privately, having promised the man confidentiality, but told Franklin that from what they talked about, it seemed clear that Bustamante knew what had happened. On the drive back, Franklin asked Bustamante about the conversation, and he was also hesitant to say too much. He said Redfield had promised to "take care of him" if he could get his personal papers back. Redfield had told him that some papers in the safe were priceless and if it had just been money, he never would have told the police. Those papers, whatever they were, had been incinerated at the Stardust ranch.

While Franklin worked with Bustamante, Officer Walter Bryson was doing a lot of legwork with plaster casts taken from the burglary site. Bryson was able to determine that the getaway car had fairly new Dunlop tires—and the only Dunlop dealer in town was Brown Motor Company. With the company's assistance, he copied down the name of every person who purchased a Dunlop tire in the past fourteen months—a daunting task and, unfortunately, one that wouldn't pay off if the car was from out of town.

Over the next few days, Franklin talked with Bustamante again, and Franklin also had him speak with the FBI. He divulged nothing further, though it was later found he still had a secret or two that he was holding back.

Chapter 8
THE COCKTAIL WAITRESS

Why the information from Bustamante did not lead to any arrests is unclear. Perhaps the police department feared compromising their informant. Regardless, the case broke wide open ten days after the crime.

In newspaper accounts of the Redfield heist story, the character who gets the least attention is Leona Mae Giordano. The reason is understandable. She was not involved in the burglary planning, took no part in the burglary itself and possibly did not even know she was directly connected to it until after the fact (though I suspect she was well aware). Her past is not without its intrigue.

Leona was born in Illinois to Charles and Ruth Melton. Her father worked as a cook, and the family traveled a great deal: Tennessee, Missouri, Illinois and Utah, all by 1920. A decade later, they had settled for a longer time in Chicago, and this is where Leona met sewing machine salesman Anthony Giordano. They married in 1934 and had two children, Patricia and Ralph.

A few years later, they divorced, and Leona moved into 936 North Wells Street. By April 1941, their legal proceedings were not quite over. Anthony had custody of their children, while Leona was seeking temporary alimony from her ex-husband. He was not about to give it to her without a fight. When the case was called before Judge Rudolph Desort, Anthony came equipped with two attorneys: Sidney Korshak and Edward S. King.

Korshak is today a legendary figure in every sense of the word. He was an attorney and fixer for the Chicago Outfit (Mafia), allegedly as far back as Al Capone and for over fifty years after. He had strong ties to both

Anthony Giordano and Leona Mae Giordano at the time of their publicized divorce. *Oak Park Oak Parker.*

Chicago politicians and businessmen, as well as Hollywood figures. At the time of the Giordano divorce, Korshak was a relatively young man. He had not yet married, and his name did not immediately create headlines. Looking back today, we have to wonder if Giordano had some sort of connections with the Chicago Outfit, but this is unconfirmed at best. An attorney representing organized crime does not imply that *all* his clients have such criminal connections.

As his witness, Anthony called his own nephew, Erco Lono of Brooklyn. Lono spoke of an affair he had been having with Leona, causing her to repeatedly shout out "Liar!" in the courtroom. According to Lono, "It began at Coney Island. She told me to put my arm around her. I didn't want to, but she said, 'You made of wood?' So I did. Another time I kissed her." After that they had "various indiscretions" (not further defined) in New York and Chicago. Lono said Leona called him before the trial and asked him not to come, but, he said, "My conscience is bothering me."

Leona took the stand and denied any indiscretions but conceded that she had called Lono before the trial. According to her, she pleaded with him not to "tell those lies" in court. Judge Desort took the matter under advisement pending a report on the children from the social services department.

Sometime between 1941 and 1950, Leona got married again, divorced again and moved to Los Angeles, where she worked as a waitress. Finally, she moved to Reno and brought her mother with her, which brings us back to the post-burglary timeline.

On the evening of March 10, cocktail waitress Leona Giordano ran into a string of bad luck and tried to use a $1,000 bill from the burglary at the blackjack table of Reno's Riverside Hotel and Casino. The money changers were on the lookout and examined bills to find serial numbers from the burglary.

Mert Wertheimer, the casino's manager, asked Giordano where she got the bill from. At first, she "pleaded intoxication" and said she did not know but soon broke down and replied vaguely, "A guy from Milwaukee who wanted me to go away with him." Wertheimer told her she was in serious trouble and alerted the police through a silent alarm at 10:26 p.m. He informed Giordano that it was in her best interest to cooperate with the authorities, a somewhat ironic suggestion coming from a man with deep gangland roots. When officers arrived, they went to Wertheimer's office and compared the bill to their list of serial numbers. It was a match. Giordano, who was waiting patiently in the casino office, was taken by police for questioning. Leading the interrogation was Lieutenant Sarah Brown.

Giordano explained that at 7:30 a.m. on March 1, the morning after the burglary, she was at Harold's Club drinking and shooting craps. During this time, she met Young, who offered her some chips, and they continued to drink until around 12:40 p.m., when they relocated to the Waldorf, where she worked, and drank some more with lunch. For part of this time, Young was joined by a "rather dark" man in a hat who "didn't look like an Italian." The second man, whose drinks were being supplied by Young, referred to Young as "Joe." Giordano did not catch his name but gathered that Young had asked him for a ride to Sacramento.

Before the day was over, the other man left, and no ride occurred. According to Giordano, at one point, the mystery man told her, "I wish that guy would get off my back; I am tired and am in no hurry to get back to Sacramento. I want to get some sleep before I start over the hill. Why don't you go after that guy? He won a lot of money and you might as well get some of it."

Young next asked Giordano to go away with him to St. Louis, but she said she couldn't go very far because of her children. She showed him photos of her children, and he took out his wallet and showed her a photo of his fourteen-year-old stepdaughter, Antoinette "Toni" Bera. Young spoke about his wife, who was at home recuperating from an operation "for some female trouble." Up until this point, Giordano had known him as Joe, but an ID card visible in his wallet revealed his identity. Young told her he was a contractor in Milwaukee and had missed his train out of Sacramento, so he would be in town another day. At this point, Young allegedly handed Giordano $1,700 that he said was for her children and her mother while Leona was gone. Over the next week, she spent the $700 around town, but she wasn't able to break the $1,000 bill until the night at the Riverside.

The local police held her without charge for thirty-four hours until things could be sorted out. The newspaper referred to her as a "dark-haired mystery woman" (other sources said red-haired) and the "mother of two teenagers." On her booking card, she gave her Reno address as 528 West Second Street. Indeed, because she was held without charge, the local newspaper was unable to find her or even verify her name. Chief Greeson declined to tell the newspapers if she was in the city jail. A reporter asked, "Could a person be taken into custody and held legally without a booking card on the public record?" The chief replied matter-of-factly, "Of course. He might be held in protective custody at his own request. And other circumstances would permit this procedure."

On Giordano's release, unbeknownst to her, federal agents followed her bus to the Alexandria Hotel in Los Angeles. When the FBI made themselves known, Giordano broke down. She said she received more money from Andrew Young and then turned over $9,100 more in stolen loot that had been taken to California inadvertently by her mother. Having moved the money to California, Giordano now faced the serious charge of transporting stolen property over state lines, a much bigger deal than a local charge of grand theft.

Although Giordano was able to identify the man she received the money from (stolen or not), she steadfastly denied knowing its origins. From the Los Angeles County Jail, she told reporters, "I don't know what this is all about. I am a singer, and my true name is Leona Mae Rogers Giordano. I am 30 years old. I don't know anything about the Redfield robbery." Either the newspapers misheard her or Giordano was lying about at least one thing—her age. Her not knowing the money's source, however, seems plausible, if unlikely. Federal Judge Ben Harrison in Los Angeles set bail at $10,000 before she was flown to Reno.

Andrew Young was picked up by the FBI on March 11. The agents surrounded his small, shabby apartment at 822 North Cass Street (where he had lived since November) and narrowed the circle. Young was unarmed and gave up without a fight, or as the press described it, "meekly." He refused to talk to FBI agents or explain how $600 in assorted bills got into

Leona Mae Giordano after her arrest, dressed the part of a Reno party girl. *Author collection.*

his work clothes pockets despite his claim that he was an unemployed construction worker. Reporters who visited him in jail described his demeanor as "sullen." When confronted about the recovered cash, Young insisted that Giordano stole the money from his pocket while he was changing his pants at the Herd and Short haberdashery on March 1 and it was not freely given. Salesman John Owings later confirmed that Young was quite upset while in the store. Adjusted for inflation, the $10,800 would be roughly $126,400 today—a bit more than your average waitress tip. Young was held in jail on $50,000 bond by Commissioner Floyd Jenkins.

Young's wife, the former Pauline Banczak, thirty-six, said she was in St. Joseph's Hospital from February 8 through 22 for abdominal surgery and her husband was with her the whole time, then took care of her when she got out. Her five children from two previous marriages were temporarily placed in an orphanage. "He was mighty good to me. I don't know why people always pick on him," she told the press. "Every time something goes wrong, they figure he did it."

Although none of the $600 matched the Redfield bills, the FBI was confident they had the right man. Harold's Club employees identified Young's photo, and those present at the haberdashery recalled him making quite a scene when he found his pocket picked. United Airlines employees recognized him, and his signature was found on the registry at the Mapes Hotel. In fact, because of the theft, he missed his United flight and stayed in Reno an extra day, creating more witnesses. Young had even approached Mr. Walters, Giordano's boss at the Waldorf, to tell him that she stole his wallet.

When Redfield was told of Young's arrest, he said, "Gosh. I assure you it won't happen again. I can't understand why they keep making all this fuss over a little thing like this"—the "little thing" being a burglary of what Redfield himself estimated at $2.5 million. When asked if he would use banks in the future, Redfield said, "I hope to tell you." Was this a yes?

On this latest charge in a life of court dates, a writ of habeas corpus was filed by Young's attorney, George E. Frederick. Young had previously used

Frederick in 1950 to earn an acquittal on charges of possessing burglary tools. Young's habeas hearing was set before Judge Robert Emmet Tehan on March 17, but the motion was rendered moot when assistant federal attorney Elsmere John Koelzer filed formal charges. Coincidentally, Koelzer died only months later.

On March 13, Michaud again left Reno by bus for Los Angeles, destination the Hotel Rector on Hollywood Boulevard—this time, allegedly, to file a lawsuit against the Greyhound Bus company following a prior accident she'd been involved in. Benton Robinson brought her to the station and later told the press he thought her suitcase felt heavy, to which Michaud replied it was "full of her songs." Robinson admitted to police he was fully aware she was carrying stolen property out of state. Was Michaud fleeing Reno after Young's arrest?

On the morning of March 15, police and FBI spoke to Redfield about the unknown woman who had given Gazzigli floor plans. After "much difficulty," Redfield finally divulged the name of Marie Jeanne Michaud. That evening, door-to-door soap salesmen John Triliegi and Frank J. Sorrenti were arrested. Triliegi, thirty-seven, of 522 East Pleasant Street, was found in St. Mary's Hospital, where he was preparing for back surgery. Although Triliegi's arrest was a consequence of connecting the dots with Gazzigli and Young, special attention must be given to the impressive gumshoe detective work of the Reno Police Department. By combing through airplane and train records, they were able to put Triliegi on the suspect list as early as March 5. Triliegi, furthermore, assisted the police by leaving his suitcase and clothing behind at the Carlton Hotel.

Sorrenti, thirty-six, was arrested at 10:00 p.m. in his apartment at 818 North Van Buren Street. He had no notable prior record. Triliegi and Sorrenti were said by the newspapers to be cousins, though this does not appear to be true. They were charged with conspiracy to transport stolen goods over state lines in what the newspapers were again calling "the biggest burglary in United States history." Both men initially denied any involvement, though Sorrenti conceded he was in Reno at the time of the heist. Both men were held in the county jail on $50,000 bond.

When asked for comment on the arrest of Triliegi and Sorrenti, Redfield calmly said, "Well, well. By gosh, that's all right. That sounds pretty good, doesn't it?" He then laughed and added, "They haven't found the safe yet, have they? Or the money?" He did not have to wait long.

The safe was found on March 16 off the Mount Rose highway, its door clearly pried open with crowbars and a sledgehammer. Louis Gazzigli gave away the spot to authorities after intense questioning. The location, at the bottom of a thirty-five-foot mine shaft, was described by the press as three quarters of a mile west of the South Virginia road and half a mile south of the Mount Rose highway, atop a sage-covered ridge. Other sources said the mine shaft was ten miles south of Reno in the Galena Mining District. Stranger still, at least one source claimed that Redfield was the owner of that particular shaft. The hole was first explored by Sergeants Franklin and Salonisen, and once confirmation was made, Isbell Construction Company came out with a crane for retrieval.

The case took a new turn on March 16 with the arrest of Marie Jeanne D'Arc Michaud, thirty-six, aboard the California Limited en route to Chicago. Michaud was traveling under the alias of Mrs. Arthur Grant. She had with her $50,000 of the stolen money, twenty-eight pieces of jewelry valued at over $25,000 and a package containing numerous securities—including 179,721 shares of stock in fifty-seven different corporations. She was brought before U.S. Commissioner Paul Pertuit, charged with conspiracy and held on $100,000 bond at the Flagstaff, Arizona jail. She reportedly huddled on her jail cot and screamed hysterically in French and English when she was not able to sleep. The newspapers referred to her as the "fingerwoman" of the crime.

FBI agent D.K. Brown and police chief Greeson were able to quickly identify some of the money in Michaud's possession as Redfield currency.

News outlets contacted sources in Canada and learned that Michaud had once been married to a Dr. Laurent Michaud, who practiced in the Abitibi area of northwest Quebec. She had apparently studied art in the Montreal area and would occasionally work as a pianist. Around Reno and Virginia City, those in "art circles" claimed not to know her.

Michaud had been a frequent guest at Redfield's home, and he told the press he was "shocked and greatly upset" by her arrest. "I trusted her implicitly." His trust was so great that he never named Michaud to police as a suspect, whereas a maid who had not been around for many years immediately came to mind.

Further referring to Michaud, Redfield said, "She has been to our house several times, but she is the last one I would have suspected of the burglary." He "[bore] no malice" toward Michaud, and in fact, he said,

> *My feeling is rather one of pity and good will toward her. She must have been very desperate to have participated in the crime—if she did—and the fact that she has attempted to end her life shows she truly regrets being a*

party to the theft. Life is one of the things that money can't buy, and is much more important than material wealth....If she has the courage to face the future, the sun will again shine for her, and life will prove worth living....It is at such times that one needs a helping hand, rather than the abuse which so many stand ready to heap upon one.

A reporter asked if Redfield was going to help Michaud fight the charges, and he said, "No, that's out of my hands now. The rest is up to the law."

By March 18, FBI estimates had veered downward, putting the theft at $300,000 in cash, $50,000 in jewelry and $1 million in securities. Some said the number was even higher, but even this $1,350,000, adjusted for inflation, would be $15.8 million in today's dollars—no small sum! After finding a note with "coded instructions" on Michaud's person that she had taken from the safe, agents scoured the Redfield residence and chiseled through thirty-nine inches of plaster, stone and concrete in the basement to reveal a hidden room—something right out of Edgar Allan Poe. The room contained 270,000 silver dollars (said to weigh nearly ten tons) and a vast quantity of collectible postage stamps. Precisely what the FBI was looking for that would help their investigation is not clear. Another document recovered was a will that directed the beneficiary to commit tax crimes: "The government can't tax wealth that can't be located. Burn this and tell no one. Carry on as though no coin or currency was left."

On the morning of March 18, a seventh person was arrested: sixty-five-year-old handyman Benton Henry Robinson, who had $36,731 of the loot in his living quarters at Stardust Ranch. The money was wrapped in a pillowcase and hidden in an overstuffed chair. When the authorities found the pillowcase, Robinson said to them, "You don't have to go any further. That's all Redfield money." This brought the total cash recovered to around $97,000. Robinson said he was a friend of Michaud's and was holding onto the money for her. She had told him that if anything happened to her, he could keep the money. The federal authorities charged him with violating the Interstate Transportation of Stolen Property (ITSP) Act. He was held on $50,000 bail but only had $14.13 in his pockets. The ranch that employed Robinson, the Stardust on Dickerson Road, had hosted Michaud as a guest for the two months prior to the heist. The ranch owners refused to talk to the press. When asked about Robinson, Redfield said they had met once at a downtown club, introduced by their mutual friend Michaud. Redfield claimed, however, that Robinson was introduced to him under a different name.

Triliegi was still in the hospital on March 18, causing U.S. Commissioner Floyd Jenkins to take the unusual step of arraigning him from his hospital bed. Triliegi was placed under $50,000 bond with a court appearance set for March 25, the same day as Andrew Young's. News of Triliegi's arrest and arraignment caught the attention of the Milwaukee County welfare department. Triliegi's family had been receiving $279 per month from the county for a total of $922 so far. What bothered the welfare department was the report that Triliegi was still driving a Cadillac. Welfare director Joseph Baldwin explained, "It's the policy of the welfare department to demand that owners of expensive automobiles sell their cars to help support themselves." Baldwin believed Triliegi may have made false statements on his welfare application.

On March 19, an eighth suspect, Anthony "Tony" Gazzigli (younger brother of Louis), confessed his involvement in the crime. With Gazzigli held at the Reno jail, police emptied his pockets to find a knife, a wallet, a comb, keys, a screwdriver and what they merely labeled "junk" on the inventory receipt. At 10:30 a.m., Anthony was at the police station with his wife, Catherine, where he made a lengthy statement to Chief Greeson and Lieutenant Sarah H. Brown, who took everything down in shorthand. His confession identified Robinson, Michaud, Triliegi and Young and pointed police to another $27,000, including a $10,000 bill, that was hidden in the basement of the Cal-Neva Club at Second and Center. Also recovered was a "sack" of securities and various pieces of jewelry that was turned over to the FBI. Rather than rehash the multipage confession here, I have already incorporated it into this story.

Although Gazzigli was with the men who destroyed the safe and had some of the loot, authorities marked him a "material witness" rather than a suspect. Special Agent D.K. Brown and Chief Greeson released a joint statement saying, "He admits that he and others previously arrested in connection with the burglary transported the safe to an isolated place near Reno where they opened the safe, removed the currency, jewelry and securities, and split the proceeds according to a prearranged plan."

Redfield was told of Anthony Gazzigli's arrest by reporters, and he replied, "Well, by gosh, that was worthwhile, wasn't it? Maybe I'll get all my money back yet if they keep this up." Redfield was not familiar with Gazzigli and did not gamble at the club that employed him. In what seemed like a continuing sliding scale, Redfield was now saying the safe contained a total of $2,350,000 in cash, jewelry and securities. The FBI insisted the number was closer to $1,500,000.

On March 22, Michaud was transferred from Flagstaff to the Washoe County jail in Reno by Deputy Marshall John Peery Francis, following an order from District Judge David William Ling, a seasoned justice who had been an FDR appointee. Before she left, Michaud spoke candidly with newspaper reporter Platt Herrick Cline and admitted her role in masterminding the theft, saying,

> *I told the men who took the safe they were not to harm anyone, not even the dog. And they were to be unarmed. I am very sorry about the shame to my family. But I was always taught to be generous to everybody. He had this $2,000,000 lying around the house and lots of other money in other places. He wouldn't spend it, and I thought the money should be placed in circulation. My parents taught me to be generous and to help needy people. I intended to use the money for good purposes. I knew the only way to hurt him was through his money….We did all this for revenge. I have personal reasons.…I planned the whole job and made all the arrangements. I never saw the men who took the safe.*

She described the dog as a "friendly dog" and said, "That old miser [Redfield] had a couple of million dollars laying around the house, besides many other millions. He would take money out of the safe, fondle it, and say to himself, 'It's all mine.'"

Michaud told Cline she was on her way to Chicago not to hide the money, as was supposed, but actually to settle an insurance claim resulting from a bus accident in which she injured her eye. In fact, she said she had even purchased the train ticket with her own, not Redfield's, money. When Michaud arrived in Reno, local reporters could not resist describing her. Now she was "somewhat stocky" with "high cheekbones" and "neatly outfitted in a black dress."

Reports also came out that while in the Flagstaff jail, Michaud had tried to commit suicide with sleeping pills. Sheriff J. Peery Francis said the pills had somehow been missed in the authorities' search of her clothes and that Michaud spent the night screaming in French and English before she "lapsed into a stupor." Her condition was not deemed serious, and medical staff let her sleep it off. Jail matron Mrs. G.F. Newman made sure she was comforted.

The press questioned Redfield about the "revenge" motive, and he said, "I cannot throw any light on the subject. There is certainly no reason for a statement like that in our relationship with her." Speaking more generally

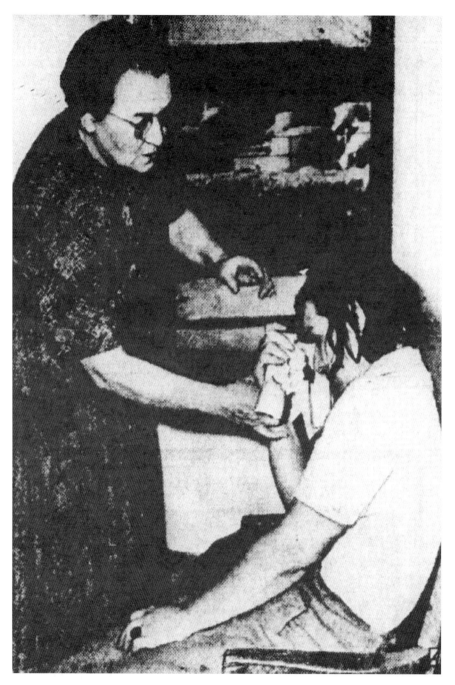

Jeanne Michaud (*seated*) cries after her arrest and is comforted by the jail's matron. *Associated Press Wire photo.*

on her version of events, Redfield said, "It sounds like she had a good imagination. But I think you can tell what is fairy tale and what is the truth. It makes very interesting reading, though, doesn't it? From what she says, you'd think I have money lying around all over the house. I haven't, I assure you." Except, of course, that he did.

With all major suspects known, Officer Franklin and an FBI agent approached Albert Bustamante once more to see if he had anything to add. Regarding those arrested, he had nothing further. He did, however, confess that he had been in the car when the Redfield home was being cased in December by "Dago Jack" and Ralph Roberts, whom he knew as Robert Lee Martin. He also now knew "Dago Jack" was actually Claude Bernard Micheletti. As far as the police file shows, nothing more was done with these three men. They likely could have added to the prosecution of Michaud, but it appears Reno preferred to keep this angle silent—perhaps to protect their informant.

Federal charges came down against Michaud, Giordano, Triliegi, Sorrenti and Young on March 31 following a grand jury proceeding in Las Vegas. The prosecutors presenting the court with evidence were Bruce Thompson and Robert McDonald, both assistant U.S. attorneys. The remaining suspects could face federal or perhaps state charges. The key distinction was whether the stolen loot crossed state lines—the factor that would make it a federal offense. Charging the three Milwaukee men was also a legal strategy on top of a mere procedure. This changed the nature of the government's extradition fight. Rather than moving from state to state, they would now be moving from one federal district to another. Perhaps not a major change—but perhaps so. They would have to see how the new venue played out.

The star witness was Anthony Gazzigli, thus far the only one with direct knowledge of the crime who had decided to turn. Redfield himself testified to the grand jury in a rare public appearance. According to press reports, he had not left his house for the previous four weeks to avoid photographers. He managed to get to Las Vegas inconspicuously by taking a bus and entered the courthouse unmolested. However, once reporters caught wind of his presence, it was harder to escape. He tried to leave through a back door. This worked, briefly, but the newsmen caught up with Redfield at the bus station. He later said they "fired a couple of flash bulbs at me, but I don't think they got a thing. It was nice to get out of the house for a few days." As of the time of the indictment, only $235,000 of the $2,500,000 Redfield claimed was missing had been recovered.

Around April 16, attorney John Squire Drendel said he had been retained to represent Mrs. Leona Giordano. She was the first of the defendants to have an attorney hired, or at least publicly identified. Two days later, Triliegi, Sorrenti and Young had a removal hearing at federal court in Milwaukee. Their attorneys successfully argued for an additional hearing on the basis that the FBI had unlawfully seized evidence from their homes that would hamper their ability to defend themselves. Until this other matter could be resolved, no removal was possible, pushing everything back at least one week.

Louis Gazzigli contacted Chief Greeson the day after the hearing to inform him that Sorrenti was a "victim of circumstance" and likely was not informed about what was going to happen in Reno. Triliegi was recovering from a back injury, so Gazzigli speculated that Sorrenti was essentially a paid chauffeur for the trip and nothing more. Gazzigli spoke with police again on April 19, filling in more of the backstory. He said up to now, he was holding back to protect his brother Tony, who had a family and no criminal record, but that no longer mattered.

On June 3, 1952, Louis Gazzigli testified before U.S. Commissioner Floyd Jenkins about whether the three Wisconsin men should be extradited to Nevada. Gazzigli testified that he drove from Milwaukee to Reno with the three men, arriving in Reno on February 25. If he made his doubts about Sorrenti known to the judge, it failed to have an effect. Gazzigli's brother Tony further said he saw Young and Triliegi in Reno "around the time of the burglary." Jenkins felt this was sufficient and passed his recommendation on to federal judge Robert Tehan for his signoff. Following the hearing, Jenkins imposed $50,000 bail on Triliegi and Sorrenti, sending them back to jail; they had posted bond before when the amount was lower.

On June 6, Michaud, Giordano and Robinson were arraigned before Judge Roger Foley. Michaud retained Robert Berry, a former Storey County district attorney (south of Reno), as her counsel. Robinson had yet to hire an advocate. Given the current court schedule, observers expected that no trial date could be set sooner than August or September. Two surprises came this day. First, Foley scheduled Giordano's trial for three days beginning on June 18 and Michaud's for a full week beginning on June 23, far sooner than anyone anticipated. Leading up to that, he also reduced bail for both women: Giordano's dropped from $10,000 to $2,500 and Michaud's from $50,000 to $10,000. Prosecutors had no objections, and even at the lower rate, no bond was posted. The other surprise came from Robinson, who appeared in court with a gray suit and a fresh haircut and without an attorney. Dale Murphy was appointed for him on the court's behalf. After a brief discussion between the two, Robinson entered a guilty plea. He revealed to those present that he had given a "full statement of the facts in this case" to the government and was asking for the judge's mercy. Foley set Robinson's sentencing for June 30 and advised him he was able to change his plea before then if he wished. Michaud's attorney was visibly shaken. With his client on the same indictment as Robinson, this would surely complicate his ability to provide a strong defense.

Evidence was still coming in as the court proceedings moved along. On the morning of June 17, Russell Smith called the FBI and had them come out to the Stardust. Multiple rings and watches were found on the property under a rock, including an item that Robinson previously claimed he fenced at Harold's Club. The value of the recovered jewels was at least $1,750.

On June 18, Leona Giordano went to trial at the federal courthouse in Carson, but the prosecution said they might have to delay the proceedings because star witness LaVere Redfield could not be found. He was subpoenaed to be a witness, but servers were unable to locate him. They believed he was in Los Angeles attending a shareholders meeting for some business he was partial owner of, but they did not know where, and calls to his home went unanswered. Assistant U.S. attorney Bruce Thompson said, "I may have to ask continuance of the trial unless Mr. Redfield is available to testify that the money was stolen." Redfield's absence was also concerning because the Michaud trial was set for the following week and would go nowhere without Redfield's involvement.

Federal judge Roger Foley issued a warrant for Redfield's arrest that same afternoon. His whereabouts had been unknown for two weeks, and authorities believed there were "indications" he was trying to avoid testifying. Reporters spoke to Nell Redfield at her home, and all she could say was, "I can't imagine why he's not here. I've checked every place he might be." She was "somewhat concerned" that "hoodlum pals" of the suspects on trial might have hurt him.

Despite Redfield's absence, Giordano was successfully convicted of transporting the stolen cash on the afternoon of June 20. Her attorney, John Squire Drendel, used Redfield's disappearance in her favor, suggesting the government had not yet proved a burglary ever occurred or that the money in Giordano's possession was stolen; neither Redfield nor Young testified to this being the case. "If the money was stolen from Mr. Redfield, the government's best evidence would have been Mr. Redfield himself— and he never took the witness stand," Drendel told the jury—a valiant argument but a failed one. Prosecutor Bruce Thompson pointed out that

Giordano did not report the rest of the cash she had when arrested for the first time and argued, "She had larceny in her heart until the last moment when she knew the jig was up."

Federal agents were able to locate Redfield late on June 20, in the small town of Sebastopol (in the general region of San Francisco). He told them, "I'll be glad to testify" but declined to explain his absence from court thus far. U.S. Commissioner Francis St. Joseph Fox signed the necessary papers, which was enough to secure Redfield's transfer to Nevada. U.S. marshals brought him back to Reno, where he was lodged in the Washoe County jail at 4:00 a.m. He declined to post the $50,000 bail set by Judge Foley and stayed in his cell, away from prying reporters. Redfield told authorities, "I can make bail in a minute, but it's not my desire. If I do I'll be free and they'll take my picture. I think I'll be safer in the custody of the marshal." At the time of fingerprinting, he had $5.81 in his pockets. On the booking sheet, he was said to be five feet, nine inches tall, 125 pounds and fifty-four years old, born in Utah. He gave his occupation as "unemployed."

Chapter 9
TRIAL

T he brief trial started on June 23, with Deputy U.S. Attorney Robert McDonald painting a broad picture for the jury of eight men and four women. He said that Marie Michaud devised the plan and drew up two diagrams of where Redfield might keep a safe hidden: either in the basement or in a closet. She approached former prizefighter Louis Gazzigli in the autumn of 1951 with these diagrams. Gazzigli and his brother Anthony, through their underworld connections, contacted Young and Triliegi. McDonald argued it was the Milwaukee men who actually removed the safe from the mansion.

On day one, Special Agent Charles H. Olson testified about the confession he had Michaud sign. During cross-examination, he acknowledged that he told Michaud of rumors that Redfield had given her tickets to Los Angeles and there may have been a Mann Act violation: bringing a woman over state lines for immoral purposes. Was the defense implying she signed her statement to avoid the Mann Act investigation?

On June 23, Redfield took the stand for the first time, wearing his blue jeans and open-collar cowboy shirt, which he told the court was his "Sunday best." He said he had given Michaud "financial aid" many times by placing bets on a roulette table for her and had purchased her a bus ticket to Los Angeles in order to sell some songs. He said that Michaud had stopped by his house in January looking to secure a loan. His wife was in Canada at the time. During the conversation, unexpected visitors dropped by, so she hid in a bedroom until they left. Redfield told the court it was likely at this time she found the safe and hatched her plan. Redfield said when he returned to the bedroom, he thought he caught Michaud going through his trousers, which were hanging in his closet and contained a wallet. "My dress jeans, that is," he clarified. "I told her, 'You must be a snoop.' Then I told her, 'You'd better not see me again because I don't like snoops.'"

Redfield testified that he first met Michaud when she tried to sell him a $325 promissory note for $275 and told him she was in the United States illegally. At this last remark, an outburst of "That is not true!" came from the defendant's chair.

The same day, Anthony Gazzigli took the stand, admitting to his role in the heist and pointing to Michaud as the ringleader. He told the jury that Michaud "told me all about Redfield and how cheap he was…how he kept telling her he was in love with her…and how he played her so dirty she was going to get revenge." Within a single day, the prosecution rested.

On June 24, defense attorney Robert Berry set forth an interesting strategy in his opening remarks for the defense's portion of the trial. He said that Michaud took the money with the "full consent and connivance of Mr. Redfield.…We maintain that the property was not stolen. There was no stolen property. We will remove some of the mystery…and reduce it to a commonplace thing. There is a good and valid defense."

That day, Michaud testified in her own defense, often speaking so fast that the press found it hard to follow her words. She insisted, "I loved Redfield." She now claimed her motive for the burglary was that same love. "If you want to cure a smoker, you take away his cigarettes," she explained. "If you have a man who worshipped pennies, you take away his pennies." Michaud claimed the pair lived "several days" as man and wife and "sealed" an agreement whereby she could have the safe in exchange for a bedroom tryst. The judge ordered all minors out of the courtroom during her testimony, fearing it would be "too spicy" for young ears. If any such spice occurred, the newspapers failed to go into depth about it.

Michaud said Redfield saw her as his "sweetheart" and explained her version of what happened the day visitors stopped by unexpectedly. She put the date at December 28 rather than in January, but the first part was essentially the same. However, according to Michaud, she was in the bedroom hiding for so long that she decided to take off her shoes and skirt and take a nap in the bed. This is when the idea came to her and she shared the plan with Redfield that would make her financially independent: fake a stolen safe, and she would have the means to pursue her dreams. "I woke up in the dark…and he came very close and tried to kiss me," she said. Redfield allegedly told her that "it was foolish for me to stay in a room downtown while he was alone in that big house. He said, 'I like to see you in my bed. I've never seen you there before. Is it comfortable?' I told him, 'I'll never be yours anymore unless it's a deal.' And he said, 'Shall we seal it?' That was consent!" She yelled this last part to the packed courtroom. "There are other ways of sealing a deal than with pencil and paper." Redfield sat expressionlessly as this was being said and told nearby reporters he had no comment. Michaud said persuading him into the deal took no more than ten minutes.

According to Michaud, Redfield asked her to stay overnight, "but I refused because I thought it unethical, indecent and immoral to make love in her home." The "her" was directed at Nell Redfield, who glared at Michaud from the front row. Despite being in love with Redfield, Michaud claimed to have rejected a $3,000 offer from him. Instead, they drove to the El Rey Hotel in Los Angeles, where they registered as a married couple, Mr. and Mrs. Arthur C. Grant—the same name she had used at other times. The safe theft was again raised, and Redfield was concerned that any "hoodlums" hired might cheat her or cause violence. She assured him that "I would send my henchmen, I would get an honest thief and that there would be no fireworks."

Michaud expressed disgust with Redfield's "miserable penny habit." In her words, "He didn't object to giving me large sums of money; it was just the little penny that became so very annoying." Judge Foley barred the jury from hearing part of Michaud's testimony. At one point, she said Redfield had visited her in jail and pleaded with her, "Throw yourself on the mercy of the court. You'll get a much lighter sentence, and I can help you later on." Foley said this alleged encounter was not "pertinent" to the case.

Whether we accept the December or January date, there seems to be a fair amount of evidence showing Michaud was already contemplating burglary before the alleged "plan" incident ever occurred.

The morning of June 25 saw Redfield called back to the stand, and what he said appeared to support Michaud—or at least not condemn her. Assistant U.S. Attorney Bruce Thompson asked him directly, "Did you tell her she could have the safe?" Rather than the expected no, Redfield said, "The defendant Jeanne Michaud...is quite a different personality." Judge Roger Foley cut off any further answer and said all that was needed was a yes or no. Redfield started again with a meandering explanation and was again stopped. "You will have to answer yes or no," Foley said sternly. In what was described as a barely audible murmur, Redfield said finally, "To the best of my memory, I don't recall it." This was hardly a no. Foley did not press him to clarify or be more firm in his denial, and Redfield was dismissed from the stand.

Around 11:47 a.m. on June 25, the speedy trial came to a close. Defense attorney Berry asked the jury, "Are you going to free her, or are you going to send her out of the sunshine and into the darkness, the same place a miser hoards his money?" The defense made a motion for acquittal, which was denied, and the fate of Michaud was in the hands of the jury. The jurors delivered their verdict in a mere ninety minutes: guilty. Michaud now faced up to ten years in prison for transporting the stolen money. Michaud appeared emotionless after the verdict was read, but about twenty minutes later, she cried as she was escorted to a car by two U.S. marshals. While she awaited sentencing, a special suicide watch was stationed outside her cell. Strangely, she shared her cell with none other than Leona Giordano.

Chapter 10
SENTENCING, PRISON AND PARDONS

On June 30, Judge Foley sentenced Michaud to five years in prison, with parole eligibility after twenty months. If all "good behavior" credits were given, the maximum would be three years and eight months. Foley warned her, "There are many dangerous criminals within the boundaries of Nevada, and it took you only a few days to find them. This venture could have ended in death. You need time to sit down and think about things." Given the limited options for women in the federal prison system, it was expected she would be sent to Alderson, West Virginia. Foley sentenced Leona Giordano to one year and one day and Benton Robinson to four years. Robinson was singled out for being Michaud's "contact with the underworld." To my great disappointment, Michaud fades from our story at this point, as there are no Alderson records still in existence, and wherever she went after that, she avoided the spotlight she had earlier craved.

Triliegi and Young were each sentenced to five years in Nevada State Prison in Carson City on September 12 for their role in the Reno heist after pleading guilty through their attorney, Bertram Mortimer "Bert" Goldwater, to daytime robbery. Goldwater was assisted by two Milwaukee attorneys, Jack Gimbel and A.J. Hedding. The two men were silent, not even saying "guilty" themselves. This sentence was the harshest that Judge John Stuart Belford was able to give, despite Young's record of murder and Triliegi's past conviction for rape. The "daylight burglary" charge was a state charge and carried lower penalties than the federal charge of interstate transport of stolen goods, which the government declined to press. They would be eligible for parole as soon as ten months later. Redfield was told about the sentencing, and after pointing out that $150,000 was still believed missing, he said, "That would appear to make burglary quite profitable. I have no doubt from what officers have indicated to me that these men have the missing money cached away somewhere." Indeed, if this was true, the payout for a short prison term was not bad.

District attorney Jack Streeter told the press he would have liked to do more, but the burglary statute did not have dollar amount tiers within it, so even a crime of this magnitude fell under the same sentencing guidelines as a much lesser crime. The federal charges would have been stronger, but Streeter's understanding was that the FBI had failed to prove any interstate aspects of the crime, or at least did not have the necessary evidence to present in court.

No money was recovered in Milwaukee, which would have been a key component to show stolen property had crossed state lines. Because of gaps in the investigation, Streeter further said he expected that Frank Sorrenti would ultimately be let go: he had no "loot" on him when arrested, and any involvement of his paled in comparison to Triliegi's and Young's. Sorrenti was being held by federal officers, so Streeter had no authority to release him until such time that he was handed over to state custody.

On September 15, the Gazzigli brothers waived their right to a preliminary hearing, which had been set for September 30 by Justice of the Peace Laurance Elgin Layman. Prosecutor Jack Streeter moved to arraign the men immediately. The *Reno Evening Gazette* explained to its readers, "While not an invariable circumstance, waiving of preliminary hearing customarily is prerequisite to a plea of guilty." They were correct.

On September 18, District Judge Harold Oliver Taber sentenced Anthony Gazzigli to five years of probation for his role in the heist after he pleaded guilty to second-degree burglary. If he failed to keep his hands clean during probation, he would go to prison for up to five years. Gazzigli's light sentence was due to his cooperation, despite admitting he was the one who "imported" the Milwaukee men who did the job. Defense attorney John Squire Drendel, who had not saved his client Leona Giordano, could feel much more confident now. Drendel pointed to Gazzigli's steady employment, as well as the fact that he had a wife and children to support. He emphasized how Gazzigli was crucial in getting two convictions for the government: he was undeniably the star witness. Drendel also made a plea for mercy, saying that sending Gazzigli to prison could open him up to retaliation from the people he sent there. Prosecutor Jack Streeter had no objections, saying Gazzigli's record was clean before this all transpired. Streeter had further discussed the case with the FBI and the U.S. Attorney's Office, and they also agreed that probation would be a fitting sentence.

Judge Taber sentenced Louis Gazzigli to the same five years for second-degree burglary; however, he was to serve them in the state prison.

U.S. Attorney Miles Nelson Pike formally withdrew charges against Frank Sorrenti the same day, making him a free man. Pike said there was "no reasonable expectation of a successful prosecution" after Sorrenti's name had not come up once during any of the previous trials. In effect, Sorrenti had served six months in jail for no crime. One wonders what his family must have been going through during this time. (Pike was later appointed the first chairman of the Nevada Gaming Commission.)

Further, Judge Foley canceled federal indictments against Triliegi and Young, deciding that after a state conviction, any further prosecution would be redundant. With these decisions, all pending court actions came to a close little more than six months after the initial crime. Justice was swift, if not completely fair.

On November 20, 1952, Mrs. Ruth Pinkley Melton, mother of Leona Giordano, passed in Reno at age fifty-nine. Although her sentence was a short one, it is unknown if Giordano was allowed to go home for a few days or if this may have helped in getting her an even earlier release.

In May 1953, the Board of Pardons and Paroles met in Carson City to look over applications from 150 inmates seeking freedom, out of a total prison population of 400. The applications were considered over a three-day period. John Triliegi was granted parole over many objections, and his release date was set for July 30, 1954—less than two years into his five-year sentence. Interestingly, at this same meeting, Louis Gazzigli's application was denied; he was expected to serve out his full five years. Triliegi had a slight advantage: the district attorney said he would be in favor of parole if Triliegi left Nevada and never came back.

Granting parole "now" for a future date was novel, so Warden Arthur Bernard explained the new system. Under the old way, prisoners would apply multiple times and be denied repeatedly. This could be a tedious task and also lower morale. Taking into consideration good behavior and projecting a date going forward gave inmates something to look forward to and reduced paperwork. Of course, if the inmate turned "bad" between the hearing and the release date, the parole could always be revoked. Bernard said while this system was new in Nevada, other states had already implemented it with positive and "gratifying" results. Interestingly, Bernard was born in Italy as

Arturo Bernardini and was himself a great example of how people could reinvent themselves in Nevada.

Other than Triliegi, perhaps the most interesting inmate to be granted parole at this time was Bobby Carter, who was serving time for assault with intent to kill. A few years earlier, on Christmas Eve, Carter was being sought by the Reno police for armed robbery. When his situation became dire, he shot and wounded three police officers in Harold's Club. Officers tracked him down to Second Street, where he was hiding behind a sign. Parole granted for the attempted murder of three police officers? Believe it.

In September 1953, Leona Giordano was out and already on the prowl again: she married Walter R. Brewer in Hollywood, California.

The warden said Andrew Young should "in no event" be paroled because of his past record. However, in October 1953, Judge A.J. Redding wrote a letter "not as an attorney" but as a person who was interested in Young's future. Redding said he had tried fifty thousand cases over his career but never saw a case like Young's. Much of the letter does point to the unfair circumstances that Young faced. However, Redding did have some of his facts mixed up. He wrote, "The man who did the shooting made a confession just before he died"—conflating Allgood and Schomber. Continuing on,

> *The feeling of hatred and disgust would affect most all men. It did not affect Young. It seems his marriage changed him and if the (Parole) Board will give him this chance and parole him, it would be a saving of a human being. I am personally interested in his future and I shall keep in contact with him as long as he lives here in Milwaukee. Should he fail me, it would be a sad blow for me. I doubt very much that he will fail me.*

His doubts were misplaced.

On May 10, 1954, Louis Gazzigli was given a parole date of March 15, 1955, under Nevada's advance system. Of the many applicants, thirty-seven were given reduced sentences at the same time as Gazzigli. They were also, coincidentally, all in prison for burglary or grand larceny.

Marie Michaud virtually disappeared after prison. In 1955, an alert went out that she was in the United States, but this appears to have been a false alarm. The search was quickly called off. She had been deported and banned from reentry once leaving Alderson.

Chapter 11
YOUNG AND ALLGOOD ADDENDUM

Young was released after serving twenty months, not even two of his five years. There is no indication he met back up with Frank Allgood, but both men returned to their old career path. Allgood, fifty-four, was caught burglarizing the Flowers Drug Store of Wausau, Wisconsin, on November 12, 1955.

Before Allgood went to trial, he was subpoenaed at the end of November 1955 to speak on behalf of Young—the two men would forever be linked. Young, through attorney Jack Gimbel, sued the State of Wisconsin for wrongful imprisonment, seeking $9,000. The maximum payout at that time was $5,000, but it could be set higher if approved by the legislature. Young maintained he was innocent of the Jonassen murder and that the governor admitted as much when he was pardoned. The state said that no such determination of "innocence" was made at the time of pardon. In addition to Allgood, Gimbel expected to call to the stand attorney Francis Lamb, who had been Governor Goodland's pardon counsel. The case was adjourned until January 3, 1956.

By March 1957, Young had been rearrested as part of a safe burglary ring with Chicagoans Lloyd Harold Lorraine and James Evans that hit fifteen supermarket targets in Beloit, Fond du Lac, Manitowoc and Appleton. This was much more sophisticated than the Redfield safe heist: they were now using electricity and explosives to get to the cash. Evans, incidentally, had a history of robbery in Wisconsin with Milwaukee

Mafia associates Carl Aiello and August Chiaverotti. Lorraine had served time in Joliet prison for bank robbery overlapping with Young, and perhaps they met in the joint. The judge was firm and gave them each twenty-year sentences.

Young passed in Milwaukee in August 1981. Allgood would pass in Milwaukee in 1989.

Chapter 12
THE MILWAUKEE VA SCAM

O f everyone involved in the burglary, directly or incidentally, the one who could not avoid the scrutiny of the law was John Triliegi. Authorities, particularly the FBI, followed him around for years to come.

For example, Triliegi was called in to the Milwaukee Police Department on October 3, 1955, for questioning concerning a burglary at Mattioli pharmacy. His friend Sam DiMaggio was arrested the day before, so Triliegi seemed like a logical suspect. However, he was released the next day and not charged.

In 1957, the FBI had each field office compile a list of "Top Ten Hoodlums": men in the area with an important connection to organized crime. Alongside such major players as the current and former Mafia boss in Milwaukee, Triliegi was added to this top ten list. His inclusion was likely based entirely on the Redfield heist, as he was not by any stretch of the imagination a major player in the Milwaukee mob. Yet by being on this list, he would automatically face more scrutiny than the average ex-con.

Triliegi was laid off by the Inwood Construction Company on January 3, 1958. He had been the labor foreman on a job expanding the Boston Store at the Bayshore Mall, but the work was now wrapping up. He was at John DeWerd's Sauna Finnish Steam Bath on South Sixth Street the next day, in a private room upstairs, when he apparently slipped and fell, breaking his left arm and knocking himself unconscious. He was brought to the Courtland Clinic. His doctor did find cuts, bruises and some swelling, but his arm seemed to be unbroken.

On January 15, 1958, an informant told the FBI that John Triliegi was not a made member of the Milwaukee Mafia but might have been a representative of the Chicago Outfit. He was said to be connected through "Mad Sam" DeStefano. A second informant corroborated Triliegi's connections. The first informant further said that Triliegi had a reputation for "peddling dope" (heroin or morphine) and that his supplier was a relative in his hometown of Omaha.

Special Agent John Holtzman observed Triliegi enter the Belmont Hotel, a notorious after-hours hangout, on February 25, 1958, and talk about horse race betting. Special Agent Warren J. Kenney observed Triliegi at the Belmont again the next day, conversing with a well-known gambler.

An informant told the FBI on February 27, 1958, that Triliegi kept in contact with Tony Biase and a man named Sam in Omaha, Nebraska, by calling the Owl Smoke Shop there. Biase was a Mafia member in the very small Omaha "family" (generally considered a faction of the Kansas City Mafia). Another informant had earlier told them that Triliegi still had loot from the Reno heist stashed out West somewhere.

John Triliegi began working as a labor foreman for Thomas H. Bentley and Son Company on April 29, 1958. He was involved in the construction of the Boys Technical High School on West Virginia Street. Triliegi was laid off on July 18, 1958, after falling into an excavated hole and tearing a ligament. Although he remained in good standing with the union, he would not be rehired on his most recent job.

Triliegi was hired as a labor foreman for the David Orr Company on September 30, 1958, and oversaw remodeling of the IRS offices in the federal building. His 1958 DeSoto was repossessed the next day by Joseph Colberg's Badger Auto Finance Company because he had failed to make payments. The David Orr Company fired Triliegi on October 14, 1958, after learning of his criminal past. They deemed it too big a security risk to give a former thief access to the offices of the IRS. This ignited a string of bad luck. Triliegi was kicked out of the Construction Laborers' Union on December 1, 1958, for failure to pay the last four months of membership dues. Triliegi was evicted from his home on North Farwell on December 9 for failure to pay rent. He and his family moved to a nearby apartment on North Humboldt.

Our subject was interviewed on June 12, 1961, by Special Agents Clark Lovrien and Warren Kenney. He told them he now lived at 2935 North Maryland Avenue and was trying to support his wife and thirteen children, who lived apart from him at the North Humboldt apartment. For the past seven months, he had been employed by the Turner Construction Company at Marine Plaza on East Wisconsin Avenue, working as a labor foreman. The twenty-two-story Marine Plaza is today known as Chase Tower. When asked about unrecovered loot from his Reno heist, he said he did not know where a single quarter of it was but had always felt one of his partners had been holding out on everyone else. Triliegi said that people seemed to think he knew where the money was, but if that was true, he would not be working construction jobs in below-zero temperatures. He also would not have faced the hardships he had in the last few years.

On May 13, 1963, an anonymous man called the U.S. marshals' office in Milwaukee and told them he was an employee on the construction site of the Veterans Affairs Center in Wood, Wisconsin (now a part of Milwaukee and not to be confused with Wood County). The man said the foreman, John Triliegi, was "shaking down" employees and demanding they give him 30 percent of their paychecks in order to keep working for him. Triliegi had twelve men working under him building the 1,264-bed hospital. This information was passed on to the FBI, who consulted with U.S. Attorney James Brennan. Brennan declined to start an investigation, saying that investigating this "non-specific allegation" could interfere with investigating a more specific allegation that could come later.

U.S. Attorney Brennan's office received a letter on June 7, 1963, from the Department of Justice informing Brennan that more specific information had been received concerning John Triliegi's alleged shakedown attempts and that an investigation was being opened. The first witness was called to Brennan's office on June 13 and spoke of his experiences with Triliegi and Triliegi's friend Sam DiMaggio, a well-known burglar and son of influential Mafia member Carlo DiMaggio. For more on Carlo DiMaggio, see this author's earlier book *Milwaukee Mafia: Mobsters in the Heartland*.

On June 20, 1963, Special Agent Warren Kenney interviewed the manager of the Merritt, Chapman and Scott Corporation who had hired John Triliegi. The man said he considered Triliegi to be an "excellent foreman" and had received "no complaints whatsoever" about his job performance. In fact, Triliegi was the only foreman of the five on-site with the authority to hire workers (after they were referred from the local labor union).

On June 24, Special Agent John Dunn interviewed Salvatore Balistreri of North Downer, a laborer on the site. Balistreri said he was born in Sicily on April 14, 1899. He'd waiting in line every morning to be picked for this job and was hired on in October 1962. Prior to that, he had worked for Seisel Construction for seventeen years. He said he knew Sam DiMaggio and John Triliegi but was never asked to pay for his position. Special Agent Kenney interviewed Ernest Anthony Christian the same day. Christian said he was born on November 19, 1905, in Rhinelander, worked for the union and was hired by Triliegi through a union agent. He had not made any payoffs or heard of anyone else who had, either. Furthermore, he said he was an army veteran who would not allow anyone to shake him down. Dunn also interviewed Manuel Duarte, of 719 East Knapp Street, who had been employed on the hospital site since November. He said he was born on January 1, 1903, in Ponta Delgada, Portugal, and became a citizen in 1942. He knew Triliegi well and carpooled to work with him. Duarte said he knew of no kickback scheme and had not paid anything for his job. Numerous other employees told the agents they'd heard "rumors" of kickbacks, but not one of them admitted that they personally paid anything.

The *Milwaukee Journal* broke the story of John Triliegi's alleged shakedown attempts on June 27, though they did not mention him by name. Inspector Harold Breier, future police chief, told the newspaper that the police had received information that an ex-convict was working on the jobsite but had not heard about any payoffs. He said, "We conducted an investigation and found no violation of the law. We turned the matter over to the FBI." The next day, H.R. Erickson, the industrial relations manager for Merritt, Chapman and Scott Corporation, told the newspaper, "We are not aware of anything of the sort, nor has it ever been brought to our attention. We would certainly be favorable toward cooperating with the FBI to the fullest extent to clear this matter up. We will be just as interested in it as the FBI until it is either proven or disproven." Peter Poberezny, the outgoing president of Laborers Union Local 113, also said he was not aware of any incidents. "If there had been any such payment," he said, "the man who received it should be in the penitentiary. Our union does not allow such a thing. I'm sure our new regime will look into it."

Following the newspaper coverage, Representative Clement J. Zablocki wrote a letter to J. Edgar Hoover asking to be kept abreast of the investigation, as he was "deeply interested in knowing the facts" of the matter. Interestingly, the Veterans Affairs Hospital was later named for Zablocki, who also had a school and library named for him after his death.

Special Agent Kenney interviewed John Triliegi directly on July 16 concerning the kickback rumors. Triliegi said he was born in Omaha and lived at 2933 North Maryland with his wife and children. He had worked on the construction site for the past year in the capacity of foreman and only hired people with the union's approval. He openly admitted that he got his sons and sons-in-law hired on to the job, but they had to be approved by the union just like anyone else. He denied collecting any payments or having Sam DiMaggio collect payments for him and said that maybe the rumor started because of the fifty-dollar fee to join the union.

Kenney interviewed Sam DiMaggio the same day. DiMaggio freely admitted to being a former safe burglar and said that he was released from Waupun in August 1962 and was hired on to the hospital job through his friend Triliegi and the union. He said he was a devoted union member and even paid his dues while in prison. He said he "would never stoop to taking payoffs" and did not believe Triliegi did either. He said with eight years left on his parole, it would be foolish to involve himself in such a trivial criminal scheme. He did admit that two of his cousins were given jobs at his suggestion, but they went through the same process as everyone else.

On August 30, 1963, U.S. Attorney James Brennan advised the FBI he was not going to file any charges against John Triliegi or Sam DiMaggio. In his opinion, the kickback story could not be corroborated, as the only person who claimed he had to pay was an ex-convict who was deemed unreliable and whose identity was never made public. But soon, Triliegi would be in trouble for something completely different.

On March 20, 1964, prosecutors told the media that there was a loosely knit gang of thirty burglars who had done fifty to one hundred jobs and had hauled off $50,000 in loot. District Attorney William McCauley issued warrants for eight members of this alleged gang: Dr. Franklin Emil Nolting, a Kewaskum dentist, accused of receiving stolen goods in Milwaukee and selling them in Minneapolis; Samuel DiMaggio, accused on four counts of burglary; John Triliegi, accused of receiving stolen goods; Harold Vick, four counts of burglary; DiMaggio's cousin Edward Harold Kretlow, one count of burglary; Jerome Morrison, one count of burglary; Larry Arndt, one count of burglary; and John Forbes, named in the warrant but not specifically charged. Triliegi was said to be the one who directed the burglars to Dr. Nolting. Some of their burglary targets were Edward Weber Construction, the Iron Workers union, Hi-Fi Fo-Fum stereo store, attorney Donald Jacobsen, Joseph Capizzi's Skylark tavern and Glenn Humphrey Chevrolet.

This news came in the wake of Triliegi's wife, Stefania, passing in February at only forty-three years old. Their many children, some still minors, were without a mother and now faced the distinct possibility of a distant father as well.

A grand jury indicted Sam DiMaggio and John Triliegi on April 13 for the crime of stealing over $300,000 worth of checks from a mail train and transporting $180,000 of the checks to Reno. The U.S. attorney prosecuting the case said he did not know why the checks were sent to Reno. I also do not know, but one has to wonder if we already met Triliegi's Reno connection.

On July 31, Federal Judge Kenneth Grubb found DiMaggio, Triliegi, Jerome Morrison and Larry Arndt guilty of stealing mail bags containing $300,000 in securities checks from the Northwestern Depot. Edward Kretlow was found not guilty.

John Triliegi entered Leavenworth Prison on November 3, 1964. He would serve less than a year, getting released on August 16, 1965. An informant later told the FBI that John Triliegi met New York mob boss Vito Genovese in prison and was supposed to deliver a message to Genovese's daughter when he got out. This story is very unlikely, but sometimes the legend is better than the truth.

After this, Triliegi stayed out of the eyes of law enforcement. A rumor later circulated that he was selling hijacked cigarettes, but he was never caught on that one. Despite a lifetime of hardships, not least of which was a recurring back injury, Triliegi made it several decades on the right side of the law, passing in 2007 at age ninety-three.

Chapter 13

THE FINAL YEARS OF WERTHEIMER AND REDFIELD

Of the gambling Wertheimer brothers, Al was the first to pass away, in 1953, at age sixty-four, of cancer. Al had operated the Aniwa Club and the Dunes Club before moving to Reno. The newspapers recalled the time a man named Harry Weitzman, perpetually drunk, won $125,000 from Al in a craps game.

Mert finally purchased the Riverside Hotel from Reno Securities, rather than merely renting casino space, in 1955. Following this, manager Arthur Allen resigned, leading to the hiring of Lee Frankovich, whom Wertheimer took from Harrah's Club in Reno. Incidentally, Frankovich's brother Mike was a film producer and chairman of the European division of Columbia Pictures. This link seemingly helped the Riverside, as actress Jean Simmons appeared there after starring in *Footsteps in the Fog*, produced by Mike. Simmons ultimately appeared in eighty-four films during Hollywood's Golden Age. The casino would be managed by Eddie O'Dowd, allowing Wertheimer to focus on the business end of things.

Wertheimer's longtime friend and associate Danny Sullivan died of a chronic heart and kidney disease in September 1956. The sixty-seven-year-old co-owner of the Nevada Club had been in failing health for some time, visiting the hospital ten times in two years. Following the funeral, his body was not laid to rest in Reno or Detroit but brought to St. Louis for burial. He was survived by his wife, Marie, and daughter Jacqueline. Jacqueline would pass less than a year later.

Mert's brother Lou was taken ill in early 1958. Although he had a financial interest in his brother's Riverside after leaving his own casino at Reno's Mapes Hotel, he left for Los Angeles to recuperate at a hotel on the Sunset

Danny Sullivan (*right*) is brought in to speak with authorities. The group appears more amused than upset. *Author collection*.

Strip. On March 17, he was visiting with his friend, film producer (and ex-convict) Joseph Michael Schenck, at the Beverly Hilton when he collapsed from a "mild stroke" and was taken to Cedars of Lebanon Hospital. A series of heart attacks and a second stroke followed, with Lou succumbing in May. His third wife, Dorothy, was at his bedside when he passed. Also surviving him was a daughter, Mrs. Yvonne Berke of Los Angeles.

In July 1958, Detroit and Reno gambling legend Mert Wertheimer died at Cedars of Lebanon Hospital in Los Angeles at age seventy-four. He had been suffering from leukemia for the past year. Mert outlived his two gambling brothers, Lou and Al, whom he buried in Hollywood. To his last days, Mert never forgot his roots in Detroit and would regularly visit old friends at the Sheraton-Cadillac Hotel and the Wonder Bar on Washington Boulevard. Though he still was active with the Riverside in an advisory role, failing health caused Wertheimer to sell the property to the Crummer Corporation, made up of Roy Crummer and associates. With Mert's passing, the casino would be overseen by his lifelong friend Ruby Mathis.

Mert Wertheimer, Detroit gambler who later made it big in Reno and found himself loosely linked to the Redfield burglary. *From the* Detroit Free Press.

In a twist of fate no one could have predicted (insert your favorite gambling metaphor here), it was Lincoln Fitzgerald who almost outlived them all—the three Wertheimer brothers and Danny Sullivan. Not only did he survive an ambush attack, but he also thrived for years to come, only increasing in respectability. In February 1962, Fitzgerald purchased the "stately home" of cattleman William H. Moffatt at 3875 South Virginia Street for $550,000. The property had previously belonged to Governor John Sparks, for whom Sparks, Nevada, is named. When he sought to expand his holdings in 1970 by constructing a fifteen-story hotel at 200 North Center Street, Fitzgerald was lauded by the city. City officials noted he had operated for twenty-five years without a hint of violence at the casino and not even a complaint about his slot machines. He was, by all measures, a clean and honest businessman—he had simply chosen a profession frowned upon by his home state of Michigan.

On April 18, 1981, Fitzgerald passed away from a respiratory infection at the age of eighty-eight. He was praised as a pioneer and a legend, earning extensive coverage on the front page of Reno periodicals. His attorney, George Folsom, delivered the eulogy and announced that "Fitz" had "belonged in Nevada." His holdings were transferred by his widow, Meta, to Fitzgeralds Gaming Corporation, which went on to acquire casinos in Las Vegas, Mississippi and Black Hawk, Colorado. Its fortunes went downhill when the family left the company. Bankruptcy followed in the early 2000s, and the final Fitzgerald property was sold off in 2007.

Ruby Mathis would remain in Reno until his own passing in April 1986. Compared to the Wertheimers', there was little fanfare, but the last of the old-time Detroit crew was gone.

And finally, Redfield.

After the burglary, Redfield lost some of his privacy but continued on much the same otherwise. His financial misadventures saw him in court throughout the 1950s, first for forcibly taking over a Reno brewery through questionable loans and later for failure to pay his taxes. A 1960 indictment said Redfield had evaded $302,847 in taxes over four years, a crime that could land him forty years in prison—more time than all the burglars combined. He was not merely underpaying but also running a scheme where he was buying and selling stocks under other names, including those of college students he met and dead relatives. At trial, he represented himself and used the opportunity to speak out against the government and the IRS in particular. Ultimately, he was found guilty of six counts, which still meant thirty years in Terminal Island prison. The judge was feeling compassionate and had each charge be sentenced concurrently—a maximum of five years.

LaVere Redfield died on September 6, 1974, at age seventy-six. His estate was estimated at more than $70 million. His will requested that two people handle the estate: his wife, Nell, and his mistress Luana Miles (the wife of his doctor). Although Nell was aware of and accepted LaVere's indiscretions, this had to have been an awkward juxtaposition. Executors found 680 bags of silver coins and 407,000 Morgan and Peace silver dollars in his Reno mansion. He is buried in Reno. Nell passed away around seven years later and used that time to distribute her wealth to charitable causes and public institutions, most notably the University of Nevada. For more on Redfield, including his connection to the Mustang Ranch brothel and Reno's seminal gangster Bill Graham, pick up Jack Harpster's biography.

Appendix

ONE ARM WOLF

When researching and writing history, sometimes the path is a straightforward ABC chronology of events: one thing caused another, which caused a third thing. More often, the researcher is taken in several different directions. One story will turn up another one, and sometimes that second story is as interesting as the first. Maybe even more interesting.

Then comes time to assemble a book. What do you keep and what do you prune? Can anything be saved for future work? Will certain stories add to the overall plot or distract? In my opinion, a few detours here and there are a welcome thing, and rabbit holes can yield pleasant surprises. Casting a wider net places the story's characters in a bigger context and highlights how many different people and events can be interconnected. While working on this book, I took a fair amount of time assembling the story of Mert Wertheimer. He is, at best, a secondary character to the main event: though connected to both Giordano and Redfield, he plays no role in the theft itself. Yet I found it was important to explore his story because it provided an excellent case study on the background of Reno's gambling scene. And just as importantly, Wertheimer was an interesting person whose story has not (to my knowledge) been assembled in detail before.

While writing about Wertheimer, I met a minor character in his story, Charles "One Arm" Wolf. Normally, this would not be a path to pursue. A secondary character to a secondary character? Yet how can you deny the allure of a character named "One Arm"? So allow me to indulge myself a bit and cover what happened to Wolf after his connection to the

Wertheimer store in Muncie. If this is not your cup of tea, skip it. Nothing will be lost. But if you're the curious type, read on—one bonus tale for you at no extra cost!

Charles Wolf came from a respected family in Hartford, Indiana. His father, Samuel, was active in Democratic politics and had run unsuccessfully for sheriff in Blackford County. His brother Perry was a minister for the United Brethren in Kansas. Charles himself was employed as a night policeman in Hartford. Most records spell the family's name "Wolf," but newspapers and government documents tended to add an *e* (Wolfe) on Charles's name. I'll follow the family's preference on this one.

Wolf became known as One Arm early on in life—some say from an accidental shooting that led to his arm being amputated. Other versions are less exciting and chalk it up to a factory accident. This apparent handicap did not stop him from working as an officer, but his employment with the police lasted only around a year, at which time he was arrested for fatally shooting his wife, Frances, in March 1921. Amazingly, at trial, he was acquitted when his attorney was able to convince the jury the whole thing was an accident. Law enforcement colleagues testified that Charles was distraught after the incident and had to repeatedly be talked down from suicide.

In October 1922, Wolf was arrested for stealing tires and hiding them at the Benjamin Arthur Hance farm. Hance was not known to be a criminal but had family ties with Wolf. His bond was posted by Dr. Harry Randolph Spickermon, a close friend of "public enemy number one" Gerald Chapman.

According to author H. Paul Jeffers, Wolf entered Chapman's orbit at least as early as March or April 1923. At this time, Dr. Harry Spickermon received a letter from the imprisoned Chapman asking for help in a jailbreak. Spickermon recruited Wolf, and the pair drove from Indiana to Georgia. On April 4, Chapman escaped out a window using bedsheets to their waiting car below. Jeffers believes this is the first time Wolf met Chapman, when the trio drove back to Muncie. While Chapman recovered in Spickermon's house, Wolf brought him books to read. Again according to Jeffers, Wolf drove Chapman to Indianapolis golf courses and assisted him in stealing a car, forging papers in the name of Waldo Miller.

After three weeks, Spickermon brought Chapman to the farm of Ben Hance, south of Eaton, who took him in under the name of Miller. Jeffers was unaware of the Wolf-Hance link, and it may have been Wolf who suggested the hideout.

Jeffers has Chapman back in Muncie on April 1, 1924, treating Spickermon and Wolf to dinner at the Braun Hotel. Chapman also purchased a variety

Charles "One Arm" Wolf (*center*) smiles as law enforcement brings him in for questioning. *From the* Muncie Evening Press.

of clothes and items for Ben Hance as a thank-you. Dr. Spickermon was picked up by federal agents later in April for the possession and distribution of narcotics. He had a reputation for providing morphine to friends and clients beyond what was proper, and this habit finally caught up with him. He served time in Atlanta Federal Prison and faded into obscurity upon his eventual release.

The Muncie department store incident happened in 1924 and is discussed in the Wertheimer chapter, so no need to rehash the details here. Wolf was,

Mary and Ben Hance, victims of Charles Wolf for telling authorities about gangster Gerald Chapman. *From the* Muncie Evening Press.

soon after, back in the headlines for all the wrong reasons. He was picked up in Blackford County for automobile theft along with Chapman gangster Kirby Davis, who was soon convicted. While out on bond, Wolf found himself in bigger trouble.

Chapman was in New Britain, Connecticut, on October 12, 1924, when he found himself in a scrape: he was approached by law enforcement officers investigating a store theft. Refusing to face arrest, he fired on his potential captor, Officer James Skelly. The shot was probably not intended to kill, but a single bullet beneath the ribs put sixteen holes in Skelly's intestines and severed a main artery. Chapman was now a cop killer. And although Wolf was several states away, this would be the beginning of the end for One Arm.

Returning to his farm on January 14, 1925, Ben Hance was surprised to see Chapman. Whether or not they knew "Waldo Miller" was Chapman in the past, they'd most likely made that connection by now. The coming and going of shady characters from their barn had to raise suspicions. And when police found and arrested Chapman on January 18, the gangster was sure it was Ben Hance or his wife, Mary, who had tipped off authorities to his whereabouts.

On January 23, in the midst of all this, Wolf was married a second time, to eighteen-year-old Lucille Strahan. The story of how they met is unknown, but Lucille surely had no idea what she was getting into.

Whether Ben Hance had been the one to finger Chapman or not, authorities considered him a valuable witness, and he found himself testifying in Connecticut on March 27, 1925. Hance told a full courtroom about Chapman coming and going from his farm, the things he saw and how Chapman would change the license plates on his car—the same car seen at the Skelly murder site.

The newspapers found Ben Hance to be an interesting case study. His criminal history was only that Wolf's stolen tires were found in his possession—and nothing more. Reporters marveled that he had never been on a train for more than eight miles and apparently almost never had his photo taken. When discussing money, he could only explain in terms of the price of wheat and butter. A farmer who did not travel was likely not odd in itself but interesting insofar as he was mixed up with some very worldly characters.

During Chapman's six-day murder trial, crowds gathered due to his status as one of the "top ten" criminals in the United States. The jury deliberated for eleven hours, after which Chapman was found guilty and eventually sentenced to hang by presiding judge Newell Jennings. The sentence was to be carried out within one year. Ben Hance, seen as the star witness, now had a target on his back.

On August 14, 1925, Wolf was picked up at his mother-in-law's house in Muncie for the murders of Benjamin Hance and Mary Gagneau Hance, residents of Eaton. Wolf and George "Dutch" Anderson were seen in the vicinity of rural Middletown where the killings occurred—the Hance couple had been driving toward Indianapolis to visit a stepdaughter. Numerous people recalled seeing both men. Mark Broadwater, assistant cashier at the Yorktown State Bank, was clear: "I have known him some time, and it was Wolf who was in the machine (automobile)." Postmaster Charles Burgess also made the identification.

Anderson was suspected of being the actual gunman, but Wolf was thought to have been more than an innocent bystander. Marshal David Booher took a statement from Ben Hance as he lay dying, and he allegedly named his assailants with his dying breath. Booher was told that Anderson scuffled with Hance during the shooting and eventually overtook the couple. Wolf took no active part in the shooting but waited in the car for Anderson to finish the job.

With Wolf in jail, Anderson eluded police and was wanted dead or alive by the authorities.

After his arrest, Wolf denied any involvement in the murder. He said he knew nothing beyond rumors and had not even known he was a suspect until the time he was taken into custody. Was it a case of mistaken identity? Was there another one-armed man? The evidence was circumstantial but consistent. Mrs. John Cromer, a farmer's wife, had seen the Anderson vehicle overtake the Hance automobile on the highway around 4:15, and it was a Ford sedan—matching the description of the car Wolf had been driving for the past month. Cromer claimed she saw shooting from one car into the other, and her descriptions were consistent with what police found soon after: Mary Hance dead and Ben Hance bleeding out from eight holes in his intestines, caused by three bullets.

Warden Henry K.W. Scott of the Wethersfield State Prison in Connecticut told the press days later that Chapman had not been made aware of the Hance slayings. There was no indication that he had ordered the killings or knew they had occurred.

Authorities spoke with the "Hance children" on August 17 and learned of the relationship between Ben Hance and the other men. It had been known that Chapman and Anderson had stayed for a while at the Hance farmhouse in 1924, but there was one more man there as well: someone known to them only as the Big Turk. This was John "Turk" Brennan. The children said they never would have expected Wolf to be involved in the murder. He was a "local boy" and had known the Hance couple all his life. At one point, for multiple weeks, Mary Hance even took care of Guy Wolf, Charles's seven-year-old son.

Mrs. Elizabeth "Bessie" Whitaker, daughter of Mary Hance, told the press,

> It was a year ago last April that Chapman and Anderson and "the Big Turk" came to this farm house to live. Our stepfather told our mother that they were federal officers who wished to go in hiding hereabouts for certain professional reasons. "The Big Turk" didn't stay long, but during the time he was here it was evident he was very closely associated with the other two. Chapman was a quiet sort—always nice and pleasant and even helping now and then with the work around the farm. But he didn't do much

talking. Anderson was the agreeable, the likable, visitor. By the hour he'd entertain mother with stories of strange things he'd seen and of the scientific wonders that he'd read about and understood.

Mary Hance cooked for Anderson, darned his socks and enjoyed his company.

With the case against Wolf less than airtight, every precaution was made before charges were officially brought. Dr. Franklin Taylor Kilgore, county coroner, held an inquest that took nearly two weeks and relied on more than forty witnesses. This was followed by a grand jury consisting of sixty witnesses. The manuscript submitted to the grand jury by Kilgore was an astounding 476 pages. An indictment followed. Wolf retained for himself two attorneys, John O'Neil and Lou A. Guthrie, with the trial expected to begin November 9 after jury selection. The defense's position was clear: the evidence was circumstantial, and according to one of the attorneys, "The only thing they might convict Wolf on is his past record."

The jury pool for Wolf was created on October 28, with fifty potential jurors being narrowed down to one dozen. The newspaper ran the names of all fifty people and remarked that it was interesting how eighteen of the possible jurors were women. Ultimately, no women would be on the jury, which is something of a mathematical anomaly if not done intentionally. Judge Clarence Dearth, the same man who handled the Muncie department store case, cleared his court calendar for a week and a half, other than fourteen divorces.

As the November 9, 1925 trial date approached, prosecutor Van Louis Ogle made the decision to try Wolf solely for the murder of Ben Hance and keep the murder of Mary on reserve. Depending on how the first trial went, the additional charge would be forthcoming or dropped altogether. The motive for killing Ben Hance was stronger, making it the better case in Ogle's eyes. Ogle said he would try the case alone and would not seek the death penalty. As he explained, "No one has ever been given the death penalty in this county, and we will not seek to establish a precedent." Although this went unsaid, it would likely not have looked good to hand down the county's first execution sentence to a man who was not the direct cause of another's death. Ogle, coincidentally, was the brother-in-law of Dr. Spickermon. So far as I know, this was never mentioned in the press, but it does make Ogle's role in taking down an alleged Chapman gang member more interesting.

Pressure also grew to punish Wolf for the murders as two literally life-changing events occurred. Gerald Chapman used up all his appeals in early November, and his execution was set for December 3. George Anderson found himself up against the law in Muskegon, Michigan, and determined he was not going to go to jail. When confronted by Detective Charles Hamilton, Anderson pulled a gun on him and delivered a fatal shot. Hamilton fought back and wrested Anderson's gun from him, returning fire, and both men were soon dead from the same gun. A crank letter arrived at the police department claiming to be from Anderson and teasing them about falsely broadcasting his death, but the body was identified in the morgue by none other than Calvin Francis Crooks, son of Mary Hance. Wolf was now the only man left facing justice, making his trial additionally symbolic.

John "Turk" Brennan was free but not wanted for any crime and was of no concern. An unnamed law enforcement authority told the press Brennan had "neither Chapman's personality nor Anderson's cleverness" and was of little consequence.

The trial disclosed little new evidence, and both sides squabbled over Hance's dying words. Fred Loftin claimed to have been present when Booher spoke to Hance and denied hearing him identify his assailants. The prosecution brought out barber Clinan Smith, who said he had a conversation with Wolf in July. Part of the discussion was about Ben Hance traveling to Brookings Lake in Michigan, and Wolf said he believed the purpose of the trip was to "hunt" Dutch Anderson. Wolf allegedly said that "he hoped Anderson would fill Hance full of lead." Lewis Henderson was in the barbershop and did not recall this conversation.

The defense provided several witnesses who saw Wolf, or at least someone matching his description, in town on the day of the murder. This included a police officer and a former mayor. Whereas the prosecution stressed that being "in town" meant he was "in the area" at the time of killing, the defense posited that if Wolf was "in town," he could not simultaneously be in the countryside, where the murders were. The defense rested its case on the morning of November 18.

Ogle's closing argument leaned heavily on the dying statement of Ben Hance, and he tried to play down all the witnesses who saw Wolf in town that day. Ogle said Wolf would have to be a "bird or airplane" to have been in all the places he was seen and noted that many of those who formed his alibi were his personal friends. One, for example, was his brother-in-law, Carroll Smith. Of course, it could also be said that if any of the defense witnesses were being honest, Wolf would have to be a "bird or airplane" to be both in the city and at the murder scene, which he allegedly was.

This group of men is believed to be the jury that convicted Charles Wolf. *Indiana Historical Society.*

Around 7:30 p.m. on November 18, the jury returned with its verdict after a mere seventy-five minutes: Wolf was guilty of first-degree murder and would be sentenced to life in prison. Wolf was visibly surprised and turned to his mother, who was sitting nearby. "Mother, I am not guilty," he assured her. Also in the room were Wolf's father, two brothers and his son Guy, aged ten. His wife, Lucille, was nearby, along with her mother, Mrs. Myrtle Ludwick Strahan, and her sister Blanche. Charles was brought to the state prison at Michigan City early the next morning. As late as noon, officials said he was still in the local jail; this white lie was to prevent any remaining Chapman gang members from rescuing Wolf during transport.

Wolf's appeal was still going through the court system in August 1926, when his wife, Lucille, filed for divorce and requested that her maiden name be restored. A strong supporter at his trial, perhaps she changed her mind. Lucille's grounds for divorce were nonsupport, which is hard to deny. On reaching the state supreme court on January 12, 1928, the conviction stood. Further, the state commission on parole refused Wolf any clemency. Reverend Perry Wolf called his brother "a kind-hearted and industrious man and a great friend of the Hances....I am positive he never consorted with 'Dutch' Anderson or Gerald Chapman."

Kirby Davis, named by the press as one of the last of the Chapman gang, started on his own crime spree in 1928–29, along with a new gang of crooks: Thomas Burke, James Waltham, Bill Lewis and Bill Bowen. Davis would shoot his way out of any scrape. The federal government wanted him for his role in a stolen car ring, and he had also gone on a series of bank robberies from Toledo, Ohio, to Angola, Indiana. On April 18, 1929, a bank robbery at Columbia City, Indiana, went sideways, with one woman killed in the bank and Sheriff Danny Haynes critically wounded. Haynes described Davis as walking with a limp—and now, he had also taken a bullet from the sheriff's gun.

Though Haynes predicted Davis would be arrested in twenty-four to forty-eight hours, he managed to elude capture until the end of August by fleeing to Dallas, Texas, and telling everyone his name was Harris. With bank robbery being a state crime at this time, those trials were delayed until after the federal charge of auto theft in Ohio was seen through to the end.

Wolf tried a new appeal on December 4, 1936, filing a writ of error coram nobis and alleging the jury had been prejudiced against him by fraudulent evidence and mistaken identity. He had a series of affidavits that he believed were "new evidence" that required a new trial. The trial judge was now L.A. Guthrie, who had to recuse himself because he had previously been Wolf's attorney in the same case.

The collected affidavits included that of Clayton Fremont Dudley, a local one-armed man who was in Yorktown on the date of the murders. Wolf said this was how his witnesses could see him in Muncie while the prosecution saw him in Yorktown. Among several others vouching for Wolfe were two sons-in-law of Mary Hance and even Earl F. Randolph, who was chief of police in Muncie at the time of the murders. Randolph swore that Wolf was not known to be associated with the Chapman gang. (Whether Randolph knew Wolf to be a Chapman gangster or not, there seems little doubt that Wolf knew the others at least casually.) Former sheriff Harry McAuley claimed to have seen Wolf. One witness said they could not testify for Wolf at trial because they were in Canada at the time, and another declined to testify because of fear of reprisals from Chapman's gang. One of the sons-in-law of Mary Hance said the man who used the name "Charles Wolf" while staying at the Hance farm was actually Turk Brennan, and he never saw the real Wolf there at all.

John "Turk" Brennan was arrested at Trenton, New Jersey, for the theft of government property on April 8, 1937. Specifically, he had allegedly robbed a bank in Lexington, Kentucky, and the haul included post office funds. This is the last we hear of him.

On March 25, 1941, Governor Henry Schricker approved the clemency commission's recommendation for Wolf, reducing his sentence to eighteen years, with parole possible as soon as 1943. His good behavior was cited as a factor. Indeed, when 1943 came, Wolf was paroled and moved to Florida, where he lived with a sister and worked as a part-time fruit buyer. According to that sister, "Charlie never talked to me about his life up north" but allegedly claimed, when he was drinking, to have $120,000 stashed in Indiana.

Guy Wolf passed in 1951 at age thirty-six. He, in turn, left behind his own son.

Attorney John O'Neill passed in March 1955 at age sixty-six. According to his obituary, the defense of Charles Wolf was one of his two biggest cases. The other involved Charles Gray, a man convicted of killing his own child. Van Ogle, who prosecuted Wolf and was the receiver in the Wertheimer department store case, died in July 1958 at age eighty-one. As in O'Neill's case, the press singled out the Wolf trial as the peak of Ogle's career.

Outliving everyone, in June 1959, Wolf died in Dundee, Florida, in what the newspapers termed a "mystery blaze," mere days after leaving the hospital following a severe beating. He was in a building with a twenty-seven-year-old man when the structure was ripped apart by an explosion. The other man was burned so extensively that he could not immediately be identified. The cause of the blast was never made public, if it was known at all.

ABOUT THE AUTHOR

By day, Gavin Schmitt works as a historian for Wisconsin's finest library. After sunset, his research turns to organized crime, unsolved murders and piracy in his home state. Best known as the author of *Milwaukee Mafia*, all he really wants is a good cup of coffee.